CONTINENTAL DRIFTER

CONTINENTAL DRIFTER

DAVE CAMERON

EDITIONS

Cover design by Terry Gallagher/Doowah Design.
Photos of Dave Cameron by Jeramy Dodds and Margaret Flood.

This book was printed on Ancient Forest Friendly paper.
Printed and bound in Canada by AGMV Marquis Imprimeur.

Acknowledgments
Thanks to Graham for believing first and most, and to Margaret for wordplay hilarity over slices of Quinpool Road's finest banana cream pie. Thanks to my friends and family for so many accepting shrugs. A special serving of gratitude to Jim and Shannon – thanks for at least letting me do the dishes. Sometimes. Thanks to Mary Jo for early editorial guidance. I'm grateful to the Canada Council for the Arts, without whose support, through the Quest Program, my trip might have remained a harebrained scheme. The good people at Greyhound, meanwhile, provided passes that allowed me to get on and off the bus at will. Not least, a tip of the wide brim to all of those who opened their stories for me between Dawson City and Key West. Your tale, for a time, was mine too.

We acknowledge the support of The Canada Council for the Arts and the Manitoba Arts Council for our publishing program.

Library and Archives Canada Cataloguing in Publication

Cameron, Dave, 1974–
        Continental drifter / Dave Cameron.

ISBN 1-897109-00-8

        1. North America—Description and travel. 2. Cameron, Dave, 1974– —Travel—United States. 3. Cameron, Dave, 1974– —Travel—Canada. 4. United States—Description and travel. 5. Canada—Description and travel. I. Title.
E27.5.C28 2004   917.304'931
C2004-906006-6

Signature Editions, P.O. Box 206, RPO Corydon
Winnipeg, Manitoba, R3M 3S7

for my father
James M. Cameron

from Dawson City

to Key West

I left Dawson City on a bug-smeared blue and white school bus known as The Agony Wagon, a nickname designed to temper the disbelief of passengers arriving in Whitehorse nearly broken after bouncing for seven hours on a stiff vinyl bench. Gearing up to highway speed, the engine groaned, the tailpipe coughed black smoke, and the entire metal framework jerked forward in fits. It seemed the bus itself had reservations about making the ride.

The unique discomfort of The Agony Wagon wasn't a revelation; the very same bus had delivered me to Dawson from Whitehorse four days earlier. I had flown into the Yukon from Toronto, via Vancouver. My plan was straightforward: ride a bus from Dawson City to Key West. Do it slowly. Be attentive. Smell every rose in a diagonal garland of provinces and states.

I also thought I might sniff out a few stories along the way. A journalist by training, I knew how the lives of strangers could be successfully condensed, squeezed into a glossy magazine or onto the "human interest" pages of a daily. But did every encounter have to become an interview? I hoped not. I wanted to travel and scribble and learn, ignoring, when possible, how I might sell the particulars when I returned home. Of course, whether or not I cared to play the role I had rehearsed for, I was still a writer: an incurable eavesdropper with a compulsion to record. Not a journalist, then, just a man keeping a journal.

In the days before departure, I had tried not to overanalyze the *why* and *what for*, told myself the reason that mattered most was as ancient and simple as the will to walk: I would do it because I could, because the idea occurred to me in a moment when I was absolutely free of doubt that such a trip was wise or realistic. I would go *just because*.

As one end point of an arbitrary journey, Dawson was an official beginning. I wouldn't reach further north than this gold rush village, which in late August was easing toward the end of another tourist season. And it was possible I would never return. Pulling away from the humble grid of cabins that was once a city of 40,000, I realized the trip was truly underway. Already the Arctic Circle was receding, nothing more than a peculiar notion in the rear-view. Already the faces of strangers were at risk of becoming indistinct as roadside weeds, the words I heard a choppy blur. Already I was facing the intimidating emptiness of my notebook. Somehow I had to pour memory into that glaring blankness, locate, if possible, the richest vein of telling detail.

There was the gold miner. I met him in the shop on one of Dawson's unpaved streets where he flogged bejewelled letter openers, key chains, and other value-boosted trinkets. The miner was clean-shaven and had short silvery hair. I couldn't picture him ankle-deep in a stream, bent toward the water with a corroded pan, or crouched next to a fire, eating beans from a dented can, his greasy beard askew. However, one doesn't wander for long in Dawson without getting a head full of such rustic imagery. Much of the town was a reminder, if not a re-creation, of the summer of 1898, when a disparate army of hardy souls arrived with their dreams of nugget-wealth and created the biggest city west of Winnipeg and north of Seattle. The initial excitement lasted for a couple of years, until the easy gold was gone. "Celebrating A Decade of Centennials," said the faded flags on street poles. Tractors and sled parts had a permanent place on random lawns. "Built in 1900 with washed up riverboat lumber," said a sign on someone's house. The humble whitewashed cabin was sitting at a slight angle, in the midst of eccentric collapse. Dawson was proudly a relic, intent on keeping its history intact, even as it sank unevenly into the permafrost. No surprise, though, that the preservation wasn't strictly romantic: Americans, Germans, Canadians, and a smattering of Japanese moseyed about town with Instamatic grins and itchy wallet fingers.

When the gold miner said he was on his way to go prospecting, I sensed an opportunity to see the country beyond the artifice. I told him I was a freelance journalist, scouting far-flung places for odd sights and adventuresome lives that might be sold to the newspapers. Though I wasn't thinking of my transcontinental expedition in terms of professional development, I also knew the word *journalist* often provided instant legitimacy. Scant worldly influence falls to the man who brands himself a shiftless vagabond.

Without pause, the gold miner agreed to take me along.

"You can help me dig," he said.

Then we were in his truck, headed west on The Top Of The World Highway. The road curled over one high brow of land on the wrinkled face of the north that looked toward the Arctic Ocean. The gold miner was the fourth generation of his kind: his great-grandfather had rushed to California 150 years before when the yellow metal was found there; his grandfather had rushed to the Yukon half a century later, and the family has remained there since (until another discovery sends everyone running). The gold miner was perhaps fifty, and in sturdy shape, his occupation no longer exacting the physical toll it once did. I asked him how the day compared to any given yesterday.

"You want to know what's changed?" he said. "Nobody picks berries anymore; nobody walks anywhere anymore; nobody takes time for the things that require time. Well, I still do, I try and use the land like the bears, okay, like it's supposed to be used. I take advantage of the lack of structure up here, the freedom of going out and doing things my own way, making things happen. Anybody can stake claims, you know. That's always been one of the freedoms up here: the land is everyone's."

He stopped talking and looked out the window to the north where clouds were staining the land in shadows. A very occasional stark-green conifer rose from the lichen and low brush as if cared for individually. The Ogilvie Mountains rose in the distance, a ridged horizon. Quietly, as though speaking to himself, the miner said, "They say those hills are full of gold."

The Ogilvie range was home to Tombstone Mountain, which appeared distinctly as a near-rectangular silhouette against the sky. Tombstone was at the centre of the most recent bitter debate between miners and environmentalists.

"I tend to think that most of them don't know sheep shit from cranberries," he said of his ideological nemeses. "Everyone should care about the environment. It shouldn't be environmentalists versus miners and a question of who's going to win, but how can we live the way we live in as sensible a manner as possible?"

Just short of the Alaska border we turned off the highway and started winding south on a steep and rocky road. The gold miner's words sounded rehearsed. His lines had the scent of something he might have shovel-fed reporters in the past. I asked whether he had ever been profiled. Indeed. A *National Geographic* writer toured a few mines with him years before and, to his complete surprise, filed a story that was less than flattering.

"It was all about stagnant water and killing the fish, bullshit like that," he said. "The important question is: what's the best way to circulate money?"

He paused as if waiting for my answer. I was imagining what the site looked like. I had seen photos in the various Klondike visitor guides. A wide swath of earth dug up, plowed over, put through the necessary sieves, nearby creeks running thick and brown. Gold, like teeth, can't be extracted gently.

The miner was starting to seem pretty slick to me, with his designer sunglasses and tidy haircut and entrenched sense of entitlement. He was a businessman in grimy rubber boots, footwear, I realized, with which he could kick my questioning ass out of his truck. I decided to play the diplomat.

"All of that tourism must be good for the town," I said.

He was ready. "That's what the environmentalists say, but the argument goes against the numbers. One guy prospecting and mining spends as much as 10,000 tourists—they don't spend anything. How much does it cost to float down a river in a canoe? They live in their RVs, make their own meals. And it's the miners who are spending at the taverns."

After about twenty minutes we were descending into a river valley. The miner pointed out the "bench," a plateau of land that had been the river bottom many thousands of years ago, and was where the gold would be sitting.

"Over time, all the lighter material gets washed away and the gold remains. Today we'll check the value of the land," he said. "If we find one gram in twelve square feet I'll get excited."

The gold miner later told me he processed about 3,000 ounces of gold in a year. My rough calculations indicated that was over a million dollars' worth, a haul that would require, well, lots and lots of land. We parked near a shallow creek and he showed me to a couple of holes that had been started previously. He left me with a shovel and a stack of five-gallon buckets and went back to set up his rusty long tom, the angular sluice that catches gold in grooved rubber mats. The process evoked another time, even if, for me, it was a borrowed nostalgia. Filling the first fifteen buckets with sand and stone was almost fun: "Look ma, I'm digging for gold!" The next fifteen, as my head disappeared below ground level, dirty sweat stung my eyes and tiny black flies began drawing blood, were cause to wonder at what cost an anecdote about how some things—like gold mining, for example—never change. The same old methods employed to yank the same old gold from the earth.

I looked out from my hole like a soldier in his trench scanning the battlefield. The low-bush willows were vibrantly yellow and orange and red, the ruby bearberries ripe and heavy on thin branches. As the gold miner returned to the river, I realized that it was just the two of us for miles around, and I felt a strange shiver at the idea of being at the source of something much greater than myself. The absence of people and their markings was so absolute as to be jarring: how far I was from the landscape of sprawling, exasperated cities. Stop-and-go traffic was difficult to imagine; the supermarket procession of maddened, toe-tapping customers was a laughable notion. I leaned back against the deep dirt wall, thinking of gift watches and wedding rings and gleaming spires. I thought of the oil travelling from the earth's crust to thirsty crowds like cola through a straw, and the raw power sent out along stiff wires from cement generators on the shores of a distant lake. Human appetite was aggressive, demanding, and unapologetic.

Soon I gave up on the fatigue-fried philosophy and started to shovel again.

Several hours and sixty-odd buckets later, the miner gently jiggled a panful of muddy water and showed me the what-for: three flakes of gold sitting in grey silt like stars in a mostly cloudy sky. All dirt and almost no pay. He said he would have to gather more evidence before making any decisions about this particular riverbed.

We packed up and took off. As the truck groaned its way out of the valley, the miner told me about his practice of flying over the working mines in his small-engine plane.

"It's beautiful land," he said. "You get a good view from up there." He looked at me and winked. "You can really see the damage."

I nodded. Grinned agreeably. Soon we were back on The Top Of The World Highway, racing alone for Dawson. I leaned back and enjoyed the subtlety of pinks being spread by sunset across the southern sky.

The Agony Wagon rumbled along, stopping at places like Braeburn Lodge, whose claim to fame was cinnamon buns the size of footballs (biggest in the world, they said, and who would contest it?), and Penny's Place at Pelly Crossing, which pronounced: "Buses and campers welcome—plenty of space to turn around." Fortunately, only a few RVs competed for room along the sporadically painted white line. We were one in a broken caravan of bugs scurrying from a barren, picked-over carcass. The hills that had been scorched by fire the previous year were blushing crimson with fireweed, a low, thick layer of colour like a scab, the first sign of healing. Additionally, nature was demonstrating how it sometimes takes in order to give: the fires had resulted in a bumper crop of wild mushrooms.

The gold miner weighed on my mind as we charged toward Whitehorse. I couldn't help feeling that to have tracked him down was a contrivance. I had actively sought a character appropriate to the scene. Journalists often know what they will find, or want to find, when they set out. On this trip, I didn't. I wasn't on assignment; there were no demands or expectations, no editor standing by, red pen at the ready. I was unemployed and unbound. I was floating, and as such perhaps I could rely on that which streamed past, the jetsam that occupied my current for a stretch; maybe the characters that found me would be the appropriate ones.

One day, after a particularly aimless wander around Dawson, I had taken a seat on a storefront bench. A native man was suddenly sitting next to me, wearing dark sunglasses and a wide grin. He had a thick salt-and-pepper moustache, and dark curly hair that was mostly corralled by a black ball cap with a red eagle insignia. He said he was two dollars short for tobacco and papers. I stood up on the boardwalk to check my pockets. I had the appropriate spare coin, and a new friend. Need is the seed of every relationship.

"Follow me," said the man as he came out of the store, and I couldn't think of a reason not to.

I decided to call him Red Max because that's what we drank together. We went to swill that terrible and terribly cheap wine on the shores of the Yukon River, within spitting distance of the native heritage information centre.

"I never went to any school," he said as we took seats on opposite sides of a picnic table. "What do I need to know that my elders can't teach me? Nothing. You need to know a few important things, not many useless things."

"What are the important things?"

"Number one: Nobody is poor when we help those next to us," he said, filling two Styrofoam cups with a fuel thick and dark as blood. He handed one to me and the cups were brought together silently. I noticed the bottle was half gone already. Red Max took a generous swallow before continuing his list. "Beware of rapid change. Stay away from technology. Pray to say thanks for the elements—all that we have that can't be owned: the sun, the river, the mountains, the wind. And include all the people in your prayer—the white men and the black men and the yellow and the red—don't leave anyone out."

He retrieved the pouch of tobacco from his jacket, and, in studied silence, began to roll a cigarette. Red Max had the calm assurance of someone who believed everything he said, someone who liked to teach when he could find willing students. He said he'd been sober for two days, and was trying to give up the drink. Sober for him meant not as wasted as usual.

"You can't give up control of yourself," he said. "We need to deal with addiction. Money and politics are addictions. You know about native land claims? They're a maze, but when you go in, they close the doors behind you; there's no way out once they got you inside. These guys driving around in their fancy trucks make me sick. They've sold us out: no understanding of the past, no sense of the future. No sense."

Red Max mostly lived in Old Crow, halfway between Dawson and the ocean, but he had a cabin on the Dempster Highway, which was his base while trapping martens from October to January. He said he wasn't going to trap the following year to allow the population to regenerate. He thumbed over his shoulder at the river that was flowing past us like soft caramel.

"With modern boats and nets the fish don't have a chance, you know? The easier it is for us, the harder it is for them. Why do we take what we can instead of what we need? You don't need much just to live: you need a little to be comfortable, you need a lot to be rich; but these empires people like to build don't mean a thing. This is beautiful and free," he said. Red Max paused briefly, gathering his next thought. "Things flow together here, they don't pull apart," he said, spreading his arms like wings. "They're taking more control, you know."

"Who?"

"Government. Other day I ran into a Fisheries guy. They're going to Inuvik to teach about boat safety. What can they teach people who have been boating since there was boats? You can't show a bear how to hibernate, a bird how to fly. He said, 'There's more to it than they think.' Fucking crazy. Once upon a time we didn't need the government: when they weren't here." He shrugged. Cigarette smoke streamed from his nostrils. "Opposite ways of life," he said. "*Disagreement* is a way of life for us."

We looked back at the main street in response to a thunderous sound coming from a motorized monster called The Statesman. The husband was driving, the wife sitting tall next to him.

"Too much comfort," said Red Max. "Everything big and always clean."

"Do you learn anything from the tourists?" I asked.

"No. Maybe. It's a culture I don't understand. Today you come around looking to meet someone like me and I get to know someone like you. Stories that have nothing in common, and maybe we both wonder, 'What's that person think about me?' Maybe you take something away with you."

He refilled our cups.

"You want to hear a real Dawson story? One that you can't take no fucking tour of? I'll tell you the story of the slide."

He pointed to the slope of sand that blanketed the hillside to the north of town.

"One time, a tribe of cannibals was living on that mountain. They were eating through the village, stealing the children, the women, the men. Eight medicine men were called in from many miles away and they arrived in a day; they were fast back then. Tough people never quit. The medicine men gathered one night on top of the mountain and started beating their drums. They pounded their rhythms hour after hour until the land collapsed and swallowed the cannibals."

He stopped to manufacture another cigarette; each roll-job was taking longer than the last. The ends of his fingers were like dry, hardened erasers, scuffed and worn.

"When did this happen?" I asked.

"I don't know," he said. "Pick a number, a thousand years. Doesn't matter. Why matters, not when."

A native teenager was crossing the field. Red Max called him over to the table.

"Do you know me?" Red Max asked him. The kid shook his head. His fists were jammed deep in the pockets of a hooded sweater. "Yes, you do. I know your brother."

The kid looked unimpressed, impatient to move on. He eyed the bottle before walking away.

"He'll be okay," said Red Max, watching the boy's back. "But the young people need our help. Breaking and entering, drugs, alcohol—these are the ways they express themselves. We have to get more camps going where you can actually show the life: how to make traps by braiding willow, how to stretch drums, how to dry moose meat, how to feed marten before trapping them. All that shit."

During a pause in the conversation I put my camera on the table, but Red Max didn't give me a chance to make the request. His upper body twitched in disapproval.

"Why do you want this? If you need to keep it, keep it up here," he said, tapping his temple with two fingers. "You want to learn something, or you want to be like these fucking people?" He gestured toward the river behind him at a freshly laundered foursome of

Westerners. I looked at Red Max as he looked away, and asked myself the usual question regarding a drunk: Is he an angry barker or a sage who slurs his wise words? I got the usual answer: Some of both. He turned to face me again.

"Something I forgot before: Don't walk over a man, you rob his spirit, and don't walk behind his back, you rob his trust."

, "I like to think I'm different than they are," I said, trying to lighten the mood. "*They're* not sitting here talking to you, right? It's just that a photo of you would help me remember this." He had nailed me, though. I was, in most ways, just another tourist, a slightly more curious cow who occasionally strayed briefly from the herd.

He snatched the camera off the table and held it in his palm like a stone he had to calculate the weight of. Eventually he found his next words, but he had to release them between silent belches.

"We're sitting here now… and you're thinking about sitting here now and having it later… permanence is a lie someone told you one time, and maybe you believed him… you can't keep what will be gone… Need proof? Proof is in the telling. Tell don't show. Tell the story until it is simple and true." He returned the camera to the table and pushed it a few inches toward me.

Even in my rapid-onset drunkenness his comment rang strangely. The opposite suggestion, *show don't tell*, was what appeared on every list of writing do's I had ever been instructed to read and obey. But Red Max's tradition was storytelling, not storyshowing. And the listener was an equal partner. He or she was responsible for image creation, for adding shape and colour as desired.

Red Max noticed the bottle of rotgut was empty. He spun the pouch of tobacco on the table and sighed heavily. His tone had been getting more aggressive, but I suspected he got truly angry only with the people he knew well, preferred picking at old scabs to breeding new trouble. In his sad, floating-quickly-downstream way, Red Max was a spectre of dying wisdom, and, perhaps, a totem of the creeping dissolution of a culture. One man can only tell us about one man.

"All last night I hear the geese and cranes heading south," he said. "Time to go home."

We both stood to leave. I promised him a postcard from somewhere down the road, and he promised to respond with some dried meat from the winter's catch. Then he focused on me with intense black eyes and insisted that we hug to fortify whatever connection had been made. And although his back was granite-hard, in that moment it seemed like I kept him from falling.

"Okay, my friend," he said. "I've got to hunt down a drink."

I watched him cross back over the main street. After exchanging a few words with a man on the bench where he'd found me, Red Max disappeared down a side avenue. Dizzy for that time of day, I sat again at the picnic table, pulling my hat down to shade against the sun. Before me, the Yukon River ran north, daunting and mighty.

Looking out the dirty bus window, my eyes fixed on a white blotch stuck to the side of a craggy black hill. When the driver yelled over the sound of the engine for everyone to look at the mountain goat, the animal took a step forward as if to illustrate itself against the rock. Humans appeared to be the rarest species in the Yukon. Migratory caribou, to the extent that they could be considered citizens within a given border, outnumbered the human population seven to one. And apparently even that small clutch of people wasn't entirely homegrown. More than once, people in Dawson told me that many northerners were escapees from elsewhere seeking a wholesale change. Two hundred kilometres south of the Arctic Circle, a person was able to stop pretending that some other life had not been deserted.

On my last night in town I had been invited to "drink and talk shit in someone's backyard." A guy in his early twenties extended the invitation. We'd just met outside Diamond Tooth Gertie's, a gambling hall and venue for can-can dancing (as well as a centrepiece in the marketing of Dawson's past). He was from Toronto, and had a summer job driving a buggy at a gold mine. "I move dirt," he explained as I followed him away from the town core and into the falling dusk.

We joined a circle of young people sitting around a fire contained by the rusty shred of an oil drum. I was introduced to various partially lit faces. They were seasonal workers, here to get a few months' pay out of the tourism industry. One girl's duty was to stand with a microphone at the front of a bus and entertain loads of visitors with Klondike Gold Rush trivia as they were driven around town. She was slumped in a metal foldout chair, recovering from an ugly day. She told a story of a broken bus and bothered customers anxious to know about the refund policy. The tour guide's boyfriend worked at Bonanza Market hawking caribou smokies (sausages) and other wild game products. He had a long beard full of twists. Given dirty fingernails and a sunburn he would have resembled an original stampeder. Another girl handled the paperwork for a First Nations land claims agreement. I asked about her job.

"Long and boring," she said, staring into the fire, and I decided that she meant both a day at work and the agreement itself.

Also in attendance was a hockey player from Team Yukon who was busy shot-gunning his personal case of beer. He punctured the base of each can with the tip of a hunting knife. Before opening the can, he covered the newly made hole with his mouth and prepared to swallow quickly. When the tab was pulled, the beer exited from the homemade opening and entered his stomach in about three seconds. One Arctic Red after another speckled his red-and-white team sweater with foam. He unsuccessfully implored everyone else to try his method.

The rest of us drank slowly, easing into a collective fireside trance. At five-minute intervals, the dirt mover ripped a few pages from a department store catalogue and stuffed them between unburned wood and the coals. All eyes watched closely as slick photos of men's evening wear transformed into a chemical ball of blue-green flame.

I stole looks at the small crowd. All of the bodies were bent, many of the thoughts probably morose. *So what if far above the rancid smoke a sky salted with stars is waiting to see if the borealis will pay a visit? A version of the same beauty could return tomorrow. So what if the visitor who has come from whatever great distance imagined there might be some Yukon-specific casual learning to be had here? What does he want, a singalong of local legends? Shall we recite, in full harmony, "The Cremation of Sam McGee"?*

I was tempted to think that Dawson hadn't changed so much after all. People came to search uncertainly; they came to scrounge for a buck. The North was just another place to survive somehow. The hockey player belched.

I didn't go out of my way to contribute, offered neither a quip nor a rousing burp. No one asked who I was beyond my name. No one asked what I was doing. Which was fine. I was a wavering flame in their lives, a flicker; soon I would be gone. The absence of curiosity saved me from articulating a best guess. The truth was my face was as wan as the next guy's. I was also entertaining the worries of itchy youth. *What was I thinking when I decided to cover 8,000 kilometres' worth of a continent by bus? What am I hoping to prove by passing through worlds unknown to me? What's the goal here?*

I had many questions for myself as I walked away from the bonfire's trembling light.

One issue in particular hounded me on the trip's first ride when Dawson City was suddenly miles behind: What had I abandoned?

There was the relationship. My girlfriend and I had been breaking up over the course of the previous year, that drawn-out and punishing manner in which romance tends to expire. It was over except for the fact that we both wondered if it was *truly over for good.* Before I left Toronto, however, I took the firm step of moving my belongings out of the apartment we shared.

And there was the promise of the educated life. Former classmates had landed jobs where they were making thirty, forty-five, sixty grand a year; some of my friends were diving into the downtown condo market. I had likewise been groomed for the workplace, coached to find a stable approach to this business of existence. I could have shaved, mailed out fifty résumés, responded politely to queries regarding my attitude, lied gently about my interest in the company's ongoing health. I could have found somewhere to be somebody.

No question I had run away. By careful design, I was free of attachments. No one had a claim on my time, or a say concerning direction and duration. No one in the world expected to see me anytime soon.

I had known such liberty in the past. About a year after completing my degree, I ambled around Asia. In the Malaysian highlands, on Thai beaches, at the edge of India's Thar Desert, I lived outside the demands of agenda, developing, as I went along, a taste for the distinctive autonomy of the traveller. Landing in Toronto (from Brisbane, via Singapore and San Francisco) at the end of that trip, I knew it would only be a matter of time before I set out again, to wherever, for however long.

And now here I was, exploring the Yukon. The range of hills the school bus was passing through included Mount Trudeau (formerly Mount Logan, at almost 6,000 metres the highest point in Canada), and I was reminded of another ragged and largely uninhabited North I once visited. While in Nepal, three friends and I had walked for sixteen days in the Himalayas. I remembered clambering over the rock piles from previous avalanches. I remembered a shepherd ushering his flock across a wooden bridge strung far above a thunderous river. I remembered trading a pair of woollen socks to a Tibetan refugee for a beaded necklace. And I remembered the sadhu.

Common in Nepal and India, sadhus were wanderers by trade whose central goal was not to have one. Sometimes they idled, sometimes they begged. Merchants who considered them a nuisance swept them along to the next square of sidewalk.

Nestled in the cleavage of 7,000-metre mountains, the sadhu gained a purity of purpose. My trekking group was lounging inside a teahouse one afternoon when a sadhu came up the trail and decided to take a break on the steps outside. A modest stack of firewood, tied with string, was balanced on his shoulders. The load would perhaps be bartered for a few meals. The man was wiry. He had a cascade of dark dreadlocks, and was wearing the lightest of cotton pants and shirt. My hiking partners encouraged me to make his acquaintance.

"Go sit with him."

"We'll take a picture."

I felt like a zoo-goer gawking at the animal-of-the-week, and decided to join him in the pen. Approaching the sadhu, I pulled a Snickers candy bar from my jacket pocket and handed it to him with a shrug, as if to say, "It's the best I can do for you." He accepted it with a grateful nod. Then he pulled out a long clay *chillum*, and stuffed it with crumbly marijuana. After taking a lungful, he passed the smoking pipe.

Despite his deep-lined face and matted hair, there was a softness about the sadhu. He sat with his legs crossed, his chin cupped in hand. His eyes were warm pools, like milk tea left to cool. Though he was wearing sandals, where the leather ended and dry brown flesh began was difficult to say.

With my heavy boots, long underwear, and water- and wind-repellent jacket, I suddenly saw myself as a member of a package tour. I was the rich, hoping to spend my way out of boredom, to draw near to the knowledge of experience, or whatever. I was rudeness and coarse understanding. I was yet one more Coca-Cola kid.

I envied the sadhu his seemingly contented nothingness. His stare wasn't stony and blank, but alive and all-accepting. His grin suggested he knew a few things that I would be wise to want to learn. After about twenty minutes, he stood, balanced the kindling on his back, and hit the trail.

Almost two years ago already, I thought. Now I was exiting the isolation of Canada's Northwest; both sides of the bus offered a blurred view of scrubby flora. Where did the sadhu find himself at this moment? Was he still walking? There was no reason to doubt it. He would walk until he couldn't, until his sandals first and then the rest of him turned to dust in the movement. Then, as dust, a wind would arrive to carry him forward a little more or else scatter his heap of particles in every direction, which might have been his idea of a perfectly peaceful ending.

In some immeasurable way, the sadhu's existence had become part of my own. About my own outlandish urges, he had been

instructive. I realized I could whittle his teachings down to one line (realizing as well that, as Red Max had demonstrated, there was a philosopher in all of us, and sometimes he cared to have an audience):
I roam, therefore I am.

We passed through the village of Carmacks. Grey log cabins planted in the dust of sparsely wooded lots made winter imaginable: wind and stunning whiteness and the reassurance of chimney smoke. I consulted my road atlas of North America, turning to the single page allotted for the Yukon and its handful of highways. There were three rattling hours to go yet. Never mind how many days and places and sticky bus stations were waiting ahead. Never mind Miami and the Keys and the idea of a satisfactory conclusion. It was a long, long way to Whitehorse.

2

One of the Yukon's fugitive citizens had grown up next door to me in Maple, Ontario. Once a small farming community, over the last twenty years Maple had been transformed into another of Toronto's suburbs. Long before the population of his hometown swelled from 2,000 to 30,000, becoming an adjunct of a metropolis, Gary, my former neighbour, decided to gather his things and flee. Maybe he saw hell in Toronto's halo, envisioned how three-bathroom, four-bedroom townhouses would sprout madly on what was prime agricultural land, low-density subdivisions being a robust and profitable crop. Maybe he foresaw the roads that would necessarily multiply to accommodate so many individual commuters—roads strung with traffic lights, roads without passing lanes, roads on which drivers must wait. Gary left town for good long before the gruesome blossoming of the Greater Toronto Area. Two decades later I discovered the point of his escape.

Gary lived in a log cabin about thirty miles north of Whitehorse and I borrowed a pickup truck from a friend in town to go for a visit while I was in the vicinity. Visible from the Klondike Highway, Gary's house was a twenty-by-twenty room divided into three parts. His wife had home-schooled their two kids, and, although the cabin was equipped with a battery-powered TV and VCR, the pair of teens often stayed with friends in Whitehorse to partake of a town's distraction and noise. The family's only neighbours were an occasional grizzly bear and cub who sometimes loitered in a nearby ravine but never stayed for long.

I had called Gary from Ontario weeks earlier, reaching him at the tire shop he managed in Whitehorse. "We don't have an address," he said. "But I can tell you how to find us."

Gary welcomed me in with a warm smile. He had long, thinning hair, and piercing blue eyes. We sat in what was the kitchen and living room and spare bedroom, and shared a pot of tea.

"The North isn't quite what it used to be," he said. "It's slowly getting busier, more conservative; there's a greater sense of hurry."

Unfortunately, he was feeling that sense of hurry as we talked. He and his family were leaving the next day on a five-week road trip to Ontario, to see his parents.

"If you go back to where you came from often enough, the changes aren't shocking. But my folks are getting old. I thought it was time again." He paused. "That's another thing, I guess: when you're here it's easy to forget about the rest of the world. Few people are spread over a huge amount of pristine land, you can drink the river water, big industry hasn't arrived yet. Winters here aren't so bad, by the way. A dry fifteen-below beats a wet zero degrees." He smiled. "Don't tell anyone."

As we talked, I realized acutely how it was our first meeting as adults. We mostly remembered each other as types. To Gary, I was one of the blond boys next door who slapped tennis balls against the garage with a hockey stick, who occasionally slept in a tent in the backyard, a kid who was always just hanging around being a kid, turning large figure eights on a small bicycle, or playing with Dinky Toys in the driveway gravel. And to me, Gary was older and cooler, a hairy mystery. He had a beard, and long braided hair, and he often wore a bandanna. He was old enough to own a used black van in which he frequently drove away from our quiet crescent, disappearing into the world for weeks at a time. He was old enough to embark on quests that lay outside the scope of my tame childhood. To me, his was a life of fantastic adventure.

Though I was young, I believe I have a fair memory of Gary's final departure. My parents and his parents and assorted other people mingled on the strip of grass adjacent to the driveway. My mother stood next to Gary's mother and rubbed her arm, perhaps trying to take a portion of the parental angst caused by this son severing himself from the family and province. Excitement and fear and hope mixed in the air, the teary cheer of necessary change. All I knew for sure was that something unusual was happening and I wanted to be part of it. Gary was loading travel supplies into the van, preparing to drive some distance I couldn't fathom to a place I wouldn't have been able to locate on a map. I recognized for the first time that a home could have wheels; that life could be transient, and something indistinct but integral—wisdom?—perhaps depended on such movement. Eventually Gary closed the back doors, and his father took a few quick photos. Then we all stared at the back of the van as the voyager rolled to the end of the street, turned left and passed out of sight. Just as the world I knew well began to seem intolerably confined, the universe I hadn't yet imagined was starting to grow.

In his teens and early twenties, Gary burned a lake of fuel seeing Canada and the United States, roaming to defeat the hold of a town whose intersections were understood. He had covered the continent in every direction, and, having visited the far Northwest, decided it was a place to return to and turn off the engine for a while. With his girlfriend, and ideas of family, the Yukon became the future.

Gary had a meditative quality. He never rushed a word. As we talked, I got the sense that listening was his preferred role in a conversation. He pressed me for details concerning this bus marathon of mine.

"So you're just doing it to do it," he said.

"More or less."

He nodded. Though I'm sure he knew my motivations well, he seemed to be waiting, for clarification, perhaps, or a revelation of character. I felt two truths in the hush of that cabin. Whatever else happened along the way, I hoped to meet personalities from the fringe and witness a few sublime scenes. I wanted to have plenty to remember. The second fact was that I was nervous, still somewhat unconvinced of the method. Could it go as planned if there was no plan other than to go?

An hour passed. On his palm, Gary turned the empty mug. He was being polite with his impatience. He had bags to pack, and he planned to spend the balance of the afternoon chopping and stacking wood and tidying the homestead. Winter would arrive before the family returned from Ontario. I stood and reached for my coat, though questions remained. I could have asked what, if anything, happened to his original wanderlust. Like Gary, I went shaggy as a young man, adopting the nomadic styling of long hair and beard (tramps like us are more image-conscious than we sometimes prefer to think). Like Gary, I travelled in lieu of options that made different sense. I could have encouraged him to further relate his fondness for the Yukon. Or ask if I might stay the night, absorb more fully the humility he cultivated here, the peace he found.

Gary walked me outside. A ten-foot-high pyramid of cut wood occupied part of the muddy driveway. Tall grasses bent south. Autumn was the most restless season, a breezy blend of anticipation and remembrance. Gary looked to the sky. Low clouds were churning.

"At this time of year you wonder if you should be leaving," he said. "That's what happens here, you leave only to come back at some point in the future."

A light rain started to fall. The day was windy and grey and somehow felt like the future, uncertain and inevitable. My former neighbour's handshake and smile and back-pat push-off seemed a remnant of the past.

You leave only to come back at some point in the future.

If the trip became a long-unwinding definition of home, his last words to me were a pretty good start.

3

Departure from Whitehorse came with comfort upgrades. I had a seat that reclined, if barely. The high windows were tinted, if still grimy. At the back of the bus was a restroom, *restroom* being a generous term for what amounted to a metallic closet featuring a bench with a hole in it. Finally, the machine's horsepower only hummed. This was the ocean liner of the highway, the jumbo jet of the road, gleaming black and white and heading somewhere with maximum smoothness. Thanks to the good people at Greyhound (and the reality of corporate monopolies), consistency of reasonably painless travel was assured. The soft grey seat carrying me out of the far North would be a near match to the one supporting me upon entry into the deep south.

I was one of about twenty-five passengers leaving town. Most of those who were travelling alone had two seats to themselves, which meant extra legroom and a place to spread carry-on baggage. I dumped out my nylon satchel: a bottle of water, a bag of peanuts, my tape player and headphones, a copy of *The Adventures of Huckleberry Finn*, and a moose tooth. The last two items had been added only the previous day, when I met the fish counter. I sat back, fingering the molar, as the Yukon passed by, a green stain of skinny conifers.

Spawning salmon know a thing or two about circular migrations and that instinct to return Gary had mentioned before we parted. Their lives are a short journey of constant movement on a predetermined route, a simple equation of existence: it ends where it began.

In my host's truck (and following his directions), I had driven to see the fish counter where he was paid to sit: three feet above the Klukshu River, near where it met the larger and faster Tatshenshini, in the territory's southwest. He looked like an as yet unclassified species of the woods. He was unshaven and unwashed, and was wearing a dark sweater, green work pants, and mud-splattered trail shoes. His work area was a platform in the middle of a wobbly bridge of boards. The platform provided enough room to sit and had a small roof overhead; it resembled a small cabin without walls.

The fish counter was the lord of the weir, which was a V-shaped fence system used to delay homecoming fish. The salmon were directed to where the fish counter sat with a net and a tub of river water. As each fish entered, a fence door was closed behind it, trapping it beneath the platform. The fish counter scooped each fish out, recorded the type, age, and sex, and then raised the door on the opposite side to allow it to proceed upstream.

"The fish know exactly how to play the river," he said. "If the water's going too fast they won't run it. They'll idle downriver and wait, go together in the evening, sometimes in the middle of the night. Not many have made it up today."

"Do you get bored?" I asked.

"No. You might think so, though. But a lot of people would like to be in my position. Mostly I just sit and listen to the water. Watch for bears. And I read."

I pulled *The Adventures of Huckleberry Finn* from a short stack of books piled on a cedar shelf nailed in place between two posts. I flipped through the novel, thinking about how my near future was full of waiting hours.

"That's just been sitting there, if you're interested," he said.

For someone who liked to lean back and think, his was the ideal job, demanding a little awareness, allowing for a lot of contemplation. I lowered the book and looked upstream.

"So what happens when they get to where they're going?"

"Huck and Jim?" he said. "They just float from one place to another. I don't think they ever really know where they're going." He was grinning.

"And the fish?"

"They use their tails to bury the eggs, then they start to decompose. Spawn and die. Spawn and die. Same as us, I guess, but condensed. They only have a few years to enjoy themselves. Once they're finished digging the reds, that's it, time to sit on the front porch with a bottle of wine and watch the sun go down."

I thanked him and walked downstream to where the rivers joined. A native man had just finished reeling in a pink salmon. The fish was flexing violently on a large flat rock. Two young girls were skipping around near the water. They stopped and watched the fish until its tail fell flat, then they started dancing again. The man drew a knife from its sheath on his thigh and steadied himself on one knee. With a single precise cut and the use of opposable thumbs, he exposed the guts and poured them out. Included in the mess was a sac of eggs, glistening and gooey. The bright orange blob slid over the wet rock and fell into a protected pool of river water as if it had its own mind to move, was programmed to complete the assigned task. The man scraped the insides a little more before bending over to let the river run between the clean flaps of meat.

Soon he was stepping back into the fast-running water. Some of the fish swam from his legs, while others, lazy with the end of life, couldn't be bothered. The backs of these had turned a sickly white, still alive but rotting quickly. Along the shore, where a few opportunistic gulls were loitering on crap-stained rocks, my eyes fell upon a large skull at the base of a tree. I assumed it had washed downstream, a piece of wilderness flotsam. The head was dry and porous, the shrunken remnant of a moose. I plucked one of the remaining molars, debating whether it made a sensible talisman. Compact, I thought. A weight I could afford.

The bus charged eastward. After going through Johnsons Crossing and Teslin, we had three unbroken hours on the way to Watson Lake, a small town near the British Columbia border. Spreading away from the highway in the late afternoon was the Cassiar mountain range, or so I assumed, as the rain was streaking the windows and a thick mist had come to squat in the nearest valley, wiping out my view.

Watson Lake was the first chance passengers had to get out and walk around, and everyone did, sighing into a standing position before heading down the middle aisle in single file. Watson Lake was notable for the largest collection of signposts in the world. Carl Lindley of Danville, Illinois erected the first sign in the town during World War II. Carl was an American soldier helping with the wartime road-building effort. He apparently found Canada a distant and forlorn land, and posted the handcrafted sign as a reminder of home. His token gesture spawned, over decades, a forest of stolen or homemade road signs: *Chattanooga City Limits, Welcome to Pleasant Grove, Utah, The Friendliest Town in the World, London, Ontario, 6,150 km →*. Those who didn't enter the truck-stop restaurant to enjoy a cling-wrapped sandwich, or employ a fully equipped restroom of standard dimensions, stayed outside and wandered, disoriented and yawning, amid this odd acreage of words.

Twenty minutes later we were back on board and moving again. The bus was a courier service as well, so while passengers rarely boarded or disembarked at crossroads and tiny hamlets, often a package had to be dropped off or picked up. For this central reason, the ride was thirty to fifty per cent longer than it would be by car: three hours became four, ten became fifteen. My mind would have to adjust to bus time, gear down to a slower, heavier pace of thought.

Impossible to forget, even in the face of my sudden fatigue, was the fact I hadn't yet decided where to end this particular ride. The ticket clerk in Whitehorse must have detected my uncertainty ("Where are you going today?" she said. "I'm not sure," I said.). Since I had a multi-trip pass, she said I could just get off when I wanted to get off, or, in the case of smaller ports of call, when stopping time was minimal, that I had to give the driver fair warning.

Before I flew out of Toronto, my father had asked what the proposed route was. We were in Kincardine, Ontario, where he and my stepmother had retired to, and where I was a temporary resident after leaving Toronto. (On the census form that arrived at their address, I fell into the category *persons with no other home.*) As a proud Canadian, Dad was miffed that I wasn't travelling solely within my country of birth. St. John's to Victoria, perhaps, or Halifax to Hay River. *Why not stay and be a Canadian who tells other Canadians about Canada?* Nonetheless, he had thoughts on how I might best dissect both nations, and one afternoon he spread a road map of North America across the picnic table.

"Let's see," he had said. "What we *do* know is that the trip will end in Florida."

A cube of ash from Dad's cigar dropped on Idaho. Several cities were circled in green highlighter, although none on either coast, and there were a few blue lines that followed possible paths south. He knew I had previously driven along the Pacific, had already seen Seattle and San Francisco, and that I had cut through the Carolinas and Virginias on different occasions while returning to Ontario from Florida. The science of my choosing could only be unsophisticated. To proceed more or less down the middle matched the logic of any other general plan. Dad took up a bright yellow highlighter and circled the name Rugby, what appeared to be a very small settlement in the upper portion of North Dakota.

"You see this place?" he said. "It's the centre."

"What do you mean?"

He smiled. "The official geographical centre of North America. Apparently Rugby is equidistant from the various compass extremes of the continent."

I nodded, not quite sure what to say.

Dad cleared his throat. "I just thought, well, there it is. You know, if you needed a target."

My father was a geographer by profession, a lifelong student of landscapes. Maps coloured many of my childhood walls, and our bookshelves were thick with atlases. We had one of those giant globes with raised topography, which allowed me to put one finger on flat Cairo and another on bumpy Kathmandu. Dad had also been an amateur explorer. Never mind the exploits of Cabot and Cartier, he might say, nothing has been found until we find it ourselves. As a younger man he referred to himself as a *Canadien errant*, which in English means wayward or badly behaved, but in French is a roamer, a rover, a rambler. However, I suspect that on very few of his own trips was he aimless—in the most literal sense of the word, *without aim*—and on my trip he probably didn't want me to be aimless either.

Rugby, North Dakota, then, was out there, a possible place to pause weeks from now. But where would I sleep tonight? The day, and my indecision, wore on. According to the atlas, we had entered British Columbia. The forthcoming curls of the Alaska Highway were pearled with choice. Wonowon, Pink Mountain, Prophet River: so many enticing destinations, so many foreign corners.

Another option, I realized, was to remain on the bus until morning, make this ride the first overnighter of the expedition. It wasn't too soon to introduce my body to the idea of an eight- or ten-hour haul, a few of which I would surely endure between here and the Gulf of Mexico.

I closed the map book. Oh well. Instinct could always kick in with a suggestion. Or perhaps I would spot something compelling through the tinted glass, a reason to hurry down the aisle and tap the driver's shoulder, request to be kindly left behind. For the time being, I shut my eyes. Gave the stare a rest.

4

As dawn flared over Fort St. John, I found myself with a seatmate. I corrected my slouch, preparing, if necessary, to be sociable and animated. Bus chat inevitably began with a single, two-part question: where are you going, and why? However, the woman beside me was so anxious to talk, I didn't have to ask.

Nan was racing to Edmonton to experience the birth of her first grandchild. Her daughter's midwife had predicted that the waters would break any time now, and Nan decided she wanted to be on hand. The bus wasn't the fastest way to get there, she knew, but it was the cheapest, and no reservation was required.

"I wonder what the baby will be like, what kind of person she'll become," she said. "My goodness, I remember when I was pregnant. There's nothing like it: the anticipation, the fear; you learn so much about yourself, about life."

"Is your daughter nervous?" I asked.

"You know what? She considered having an abortion."

Nan said her son-in-law apparently wasn't sure he wanted a child, which caused similar wheels of doubt to start turning in her daughter's mind.

"But then she called one night and said, 'Mom, it's okay, it's going to be okay.' Sheesh. I started crying so that I couldn't even talk. My goodness, I was a wreck for a week wondering if she was going to kill that baby. Being a parent is a hard thing, I know that, and any child who isn't welcome into this world will suffer, that I also know."

Nan's hair was a puffy silver cloud, and her face was smooth and unmarked, younger than most of the faces that accompany such hair. She paused long enough to take a deep breath. Life with her own mother had been far from ideal. "When I was a kid coming home from school I didn't get a 'How was your day, sweetie?' I got a smack across the face. But I came to understand that she wasn't mad at me, I was just an easy outlet for the problems she was having."

"Your father—"

"Simple," she said. "Mom was *his* punching bag. I'd listen from my bedroom with my eyes shut tight, fists clenched like this. I remember wondering if that was how an earthquake felt. I kept listening, and before long there was nothing, just absolute silence, and the silence came suddenly, you know, like a giant crack had opened in the earth and swallowed us whole."

She nodded at me with raised eyebrows as if she was surprised at herself, had never described it so perfectly before. I also raised my eyebrows. She smiled and put her hand on my knee.

"Sorry to dump that on you," she said.

I grinned, a substitute for the appropriately sensitive comment I couldn't quite locate.

"I'll shut my loud mouth now," said Nan. "Are you on holiday or—"

The buried twitter of a cellphone interrupted her, and, pulling the slim silver device from her handbag, she switched smoothly to another conversation.

"Hello... Hey, what's up?... I'm on the bus right now... I'm not sure exactly, early afternoon... Uh huh... Yeah, what's he want?... Gimme a break..."

Nan smiled at me and shook her head as if to indicate she couldn't believe what she was hearing.

"Well, what does he expect?... Exactly..." (Giggling.) "Awright... Okay... Ciao." She folded the phone and rolled her eyes at me. "Where are you, he wants to know," she said. "I've barely left."

I stifled a yawn. "I guess Dawson Creek is next."

"Is that where you live?" she asked.

"No. I thought I might get off there."

"You might, huh?" she said. "It's still up in the air."

I nodded. She smiled, and leaned away from me as though to get a more complete look. Boarding a long-distance bus, you can be anyone at all; nobody knows you, your history or hopes or hang-ups. Every ride is like the first page of a fictional life. I wondered what Nan was guessing about me, which shard of mass culture informed her impressions of restless youth. Was I an unfortunate orphan? Did I flirt with crime? "You're a quiet one, aren't you?" she said at one point, and I thought my turn had come to spin a yarn, to reduce my narrative to some palatable essence. I didn't tell Nan that she was in the running to become a part of my story. I didn't discuss how I might borrow her wishes and sorrow, or which of her life's lines I would carry with me long after we parted ways.

"What do you listen to?" she said when she noticed my cassette player.

"Dylan's in there now."

"Bob Dylan. Sheesh. 'The Tambourine Man' and that. I knew all his songs when I was your age. Neil Young, Jimi Hendrix, all that stuff. I listen to Christian rock now."

Ah. Born-again. I realized that she likely used to say shit instead of sheesh, God rather than goodness. Or maybe she had just made the linguistic transition from mother to grandmother. If Nan wasn't talking, she was nibbling on food. At regular intervals she offered me some of her chocolate-type candy, chips, and crackers, all of which, I noticed, were "sensible snack" products. She was a client consultant for a weight-loss program. After shedding forty pounds herself, she became such a devout believer that she was hired on to convince and encourage others. Then we skipped headlong into her trials with marriage. Nan was twice divorced. Her first husband cheated on her with her sister, and later cheated on her sister with another woman.

"The second gal was how I was able to forgive my sister," she said. "It didn't have anything to do with her at all. He was always chasing something new, something different, something better that was actually worse. You know: I'm talking too much."

"No, you're not," I said. She looked at my earphones. "Do you want a refresher course?" I said, lifting the mini stereo toward her.

"Oh, sure," she said. "Maybe just a song."

...take me for a trip upon your magic swirling ship...

My feet touched ground in Dawson Creek, where the prairie swam east in waves, where an unfriendly September wind made my eyes water, where I knew not a soul. I pulled my backpack from the bus's hollow underbelly, and took aim at the town centre.

I took a room at Dawson Creek's Alaska Hotel, one block down from a strip joint called The Cage, and mere steps from the monument that marked mile zero of the Alaska Highway. From my window I could see tourists—"from as far away as Texas!" according to the info kiosk teenager—taking a quick photo of the peeling white obelisk before getting back into their campers to head either northwest or southeast.

The Alaska was quaintly imperfect. The shared washroom didn't have a light, my slanted bedroom featured a rusty, tap-dripping sink next to the sagging bed, and a dusty and toothless stuffed beaver stood on guard in the hallway, all of which added up to "charming and historic accommodation." At least charming and historic came cheap—eighty-five bucks for a week, about what I would have spent in one night at any of the highway hotels.

After unzipping its many pockets, I dumped the entire contents of my backpack onto the bed, thinking I might carry out a quick reorganization. Dirty laundry became a pile by the door; clean clothes I refolded and set on the floor. I put the atlas, my notebook, and my toiletries on the bedside table. Mostly what remained was a jumble of tools: an extra pen, two books of matches, a jackknife, a small flashlight, a flask (half full of rye), and a small sewing kit. I thought: It's as if I'm expecting to get lost in the woods.

And then I remembered my father's compass. I had hardly considered it since I left Toronto. Where was it? I grabbed my pack and started feeling around—the thing had a ridiculous number of nooks and crannies—and there, at the bottom of a narrow side pocket, was the wool sock in which I had wrapped the old silver compass. It had slipped below the backpack's removable waterproof cover, which was bunched up in the same sleeve. Relieved, I set the compass on my notebook, and finished tidying.

Once the bed was cleared, I shoved it toward the window to widen my view of the sky. If this was going to be home for a time, I wanted to get comfortable. I stretched out and watched the clouds hurry and change. I opened the compass, held it a couple of inches above my rib cage. As the pointer pointed (was it trembling or was I?), I remembered again that planning session by the picnic table in Kincardine.

Eventually, Dad had put the cap on his yellow highlighter and folded the map of North America. Before we went inside, he reached into the chest pocket of his shirt, and offered me the round instrument. "It's yours," he said.

"Yeah?"

"I don't need it. I don't wander much these days."

I'm sure he didn't think I needed a compass, either, not on this trip of well-signed highways. He just wanted to send me off with a reasonably portable token of support. Dad had tried to downplay his gift with a wink and a line. "Just remember," he said, "you still have to know where you came from and where you want to go."

Though there was no call for a plan, an approximate itinerary, at least for the next several days, was establishing itself in my mind. I had a friend in Edmonton, and an uncle in Red Deer. While both parties knew I was headed in the general direction of Alberta, neither expected me to drop by absolutely. But the attraction for me was obvious: familiar faces behind an open door, agreeable smells wafting from the kitchen, bathroom soap carved like a rose. Why veer from the fertile promise of hospitality? I would roll over to Highway 2, and hit two cities that would be happy to have me. Knowing the week ahead was agenda enough.

The Cage had dancers working the weekday lunch hour. This struck me as unlikely for what seemed a subdued mid-sized town (every citizen who arrived on Dawson Creek's main street went about his or her business with calm deliberation: entering the post office to get the mail, entering the bank to check debts, entering the café to get a coffee). And it was simply true there wasn't much else to do.

Entering the basement tavern, my eyes had to adjust from day. Most of the available light was coming from a few neon beer signs and the string of small white lights running around the perimeter of the stage. A faux-blonde lady was busy entertaining in the dungeon-dark, her bikinied bottom resting on a swing that was an aluminum bar hanging from two chains.

I shuffled toward the glow cast by the bar.

Over the course of two more songs the blonde peeled off what remained of her last layer. She had a boyish body, small, undeveloped, plump in parts. A black, mushroom-shaped bruise decorated the back of one thigh. She made sure the audience of eight got a good look at every angle of her melancholy bareness; I felt like a medical intern who would later have to suggest to the patient what might be wrong with her. A DJ eventually voiced in from his corner barracks: "Once again, ladies and gents: Nikkita Star. Put your hands together!" She left the stage to a smattering of applause. The crowd was a mix of husbands and wives, boyfriends and girlfriends, all of whom seemed unsurprised that the club sandwich came with a side order of nude ballet.

Beneath the chalkboard "specials" menu, Nikkita Star was getting dressed as casually as if she were alone in her bedroom, palming her tiny breasts, fixing her hair, and stepping into a pair of jeans. Once comfortable, she came over to the bar, dropping a pair of rollerblades at the foot of the stool next to mine. When she ordered a beer, I thought I heard an accent.

"Can I ask where you're from?" I said.

"You can ask anything you want," she said, lighting a cigarette. She grinned. "Texas. Shelby, Texas. It's an Aryan Nation town. You know, small and tough. Angry."

"I assume Nikkita is a stage name."

"My real name's Nikki, see, N-I-K-K-I, so Nikkita is just my name plus tits and ass. Get it?"

Nikki had started stripping in Toronto six months before, and was now working a loop of towns that included Fort St. John, Grande Prairie, Dawson Creek, and Red Deer. During each stint, she split an apartment with another dancer.

"You start to think of these towns as home," she said. "Eventually you can't tell them apart."

She had, however, worked a week in Yellowknife, which was unusual for two reasons.

"Smaller and colder," she shrugged. "You know, I've had pneumonia, like, five times in Canada. I always wear a sweater. I don't think my body will ever adjust to the weather. After Yellowknife they wanted me to go to Inuvik, which is, like, another four hours straight up. I told them to forget it."

She sucked on her smoke and exhaled out of the side of her mouth.

"But you get addicted to the money, so even though you're worn out and it's not good for your body, you don't stop."

She was making sixty-five bucks per three-song set, three grand in a good week. If and when she returned to the U.S. she wanted to go back to school. One more year of training and she would have her journeyman's papers for sheet metal work. When she held out her hands to me, I expected to see evidence of blue-collar labour. But they were pale and dainty, like a young girl's, the nails painted sloppily with polish the colour of grape bubble gum.

"Eventually I'll make it to Vancouver," she said. "I hear it's nice there."

"Then home?"

"Sure. No rush. Home ain't going nowhere."

Nikki stared at the row of liquor bottles above the cash register. I was curious about Texas and her youth. I wanted a few brutal particulars. Did she think she would stick to her skeletal dreams? In my fear of being seen as desperate, as unpredictable, as a creep who tries to pick up at nudie bars, no questions came. We drank side by side in silence.

"Hey," she said. "Do you know anything about cooking a turkey?"

"Very little," I said.

"I've got one in the oven right now, and I have no idea when it should be done." She took a swallow from her Budweiser. Eyed me. "If I brought you over to look at it, do you think you'd know? You could eat with us."

I smiled. "I could help you guess."

She seemed to be considering the idea for real. My day flowered with potential weirdness. "You know what?" she said. "My roommate wouldn't go for this at all. Sorry."

Nikki slid off the stool, and bent at the waist to put on her rollerblades. Then she was gone, skating smoothly to the exit, leaving me at the bar with my third beer and the sensation of events failing to ensue. Not that I felt extreme loss, or cheated out of the promise of quirky romance. I hadn't been thinking seduction. I wasn't feeling randy in the least. Nikki's suggestion had exceeded my imaginative capabilities. I *almost* sat down to turkey dinner with a stripper. Nuts.

Had I stayed at The Cage, I might have spiralled toward daytime drunkenness. I wasn't sad. I had nothing specific to mourn. Nonetheless, there was an absence, an ambiguous hole, and I felt at risk of becoming a sour-mouthed nobody tripping up the street confirming the permanence of his misery. I left the bar as another young woman began to jiggle her B-cups below desolate beams of pale light.

Dawson Creek's residential grid was serene on this weekday afternoon, brick bungalows and trim front yards occasionally lit by the sun of a partly cloudy sky. I walked several blocks in a few different directions, as if, sooner or later, I would somehow outpace my underlying loneliness. I spotted a payphone outside a convenience store, and gave in to the urge to talk to someone who knew me well.

My last relationship had been marked by my departures and arrivals. I would go away for months at a stretch, occupying myself in Japan, Australia, Western Canada. My girlfriend said she didn't mind that pattern as long as she knew when she would see me again. On one occasion she joined me in Greece. When she went home, I travelled on to Turkey, returning to Toronto five weeks later. The boomeranging worked okay for a time. I always came back to known satisfactions.

A couple of months prior to leaving for Whitehorse, I told her that she should no longer count on me, and that I would be moving out of the Toronto apartment we had occupied together for three years. I started collecting my portion of the junk that weighs all of us down, hauling it to a selection of family attics and basements in southern Ontario. Nonetheless, the true termination of what we were dragged on. *The End* was still in progress.

She answered after three rings.

"Hi," I said.

"Hi."

"I just wanted to say hi."

She asked me how the trip was going, if I was meeting unique people, where I thought I might be tomorrow. During this inoffensive, pedestrian exchange, I remembered our most recent face-to-face. We had sat down to the last supper: rotini, garlic bread, wine. Some of my belongings lay scattered around the living room. I had yet to pack up whichever music and books I thought were mine, avoiding the dreaded division of ownership.

"Where would you rather be right now?" she had asked, pushing around her pasta.

Anywhere else in the world, I thought. The scene was needlessly awful for both of us. I said nothing.

"You always want to be somewhere else, don't you?"

"Not exactly," I said. "I'm not easily satisfied."

She glared at me. "What are you afraid of?"

"Nothing," I said. A lie. I was a tidy stereotype, heterosexual male, 25-34, rootless and marriage-wary, actively avoiding what the lifestyle magazines and self-help programs called commitment. Of course I was afraid. I was fearful of the inevitabilities I thought would be associated with constancy, such as tedium, frustration, and resentment. I thought the framework of a future that was under quiet construction around me looked rickety, a weak-jointed scaffold of expectations and unspoken strategy.

As content as my girlfriend claimed to be, I think she conceived of a more bountiful arrangement. Classmates from high school were swapping rings and vows; pregnancies were being announced with increasing frequency. Nothing makes a girl anxious like other girls becoming women in certain ways.

While there may be consolation in common goals, only a fool would promise the future to some other soul.

I resolved to leave her. I left.

Now I watched as a Dawson Creeker drank half a litre of chocolate milk in one long gulp. He tossed the plastic container like a basketball into the nearest garbage can, got back into his truck, and exited the parking lot loudly, with the back tires smoking.

"This is strange, isn't it?" said my ex. "When you were in India and Nepal you were far away and completely out of touch. And now you're closer but further gone."

"That is strange," I said.

On that grim last night in Toronto I suggested she might find my absence a relief, that to have her wait patiently (as she already had) for me to get back every time was unfair. For a guy who preferred to roam on his own, thinking minimally about eventual homecomings, that reasoning was problematic. Frantic for healing words, I had ended up being merely patronizing.

I shifted my weight, took two steps in order to lean on the opposite side of the booth. The conversation bumped along, a drawn-out dialogue during which I stuttered and stammered. Juggled pointless banalities. Waited. Questions surfaced as I stared over the rolling prairie at a freshly painted green and white silo, my phone ear tingling from being pinched against my shoulder. Do I travel to collect things or to discard them? Is the wandering life, despite its many and easy poetic justifications, simply a convenient excuse to stay away?

A teenage girl had been looking around the corner at me at five-minute intervals, her expression one of increasing dismay and impatience. Eventually she decided to hold her gaze and stared at me, into me, with squinting eyes, as if to cast a vote on my fate. I turned my back to her.

I cleared my throat.

"You can't always be the passive observer, you know," said my ex. "Sometimes you have to participate. You have to be one of your own characters. You have to be the *main* character."

"I'm most comfortable on the outside looking in," I said.

"Is there any emotion on the outside? Is there any real life?"

"All of it is real life. Just not mine." I couldn't suppress a small laugh.

"Exactly. You're like a pair of eyes without a body. Floating eyes."

"Detached retinas, you might say."

"Definitely detached," she said. "Someday I might understand you."

"When you figure me out, let me know."

The time was past for guilty, repetitive apologies. Again, I could be the frustrating and sometimes witty guy she was doomed to desire. As we said our goodbyes, I realized I hadn't gotten what I was looking for—an effortless connection. I *might* understand you, she had said. *Someday.*

Wasn't it time to stop kidding ourselves?

I returned to the bluster of a day that felt stripped of all specificity. A pair of pickup trucks screeched past in tandem. The sky seemed headed for a peachy sunset even as it included a few dark, heavy clouds suspended here and there, portents of dreariness.

Appearing nightly at the Alaska's street level tavern was a band called Hughie & Co. Hughie himself, who was both singer and lead guitarist, lived down the hall from me during his gig. He was from Surrey, B.C., and was working the road like Nikkita Star, trying to enliven the bar crowds of mid-sized towns two weeks at a time. The band played only covers, rock standards lodged in the collective memory of at least two generations. As my bedroom was directly above the stage, I often couldn't help but hum along.

Hughie was in his early thirties and suffering premature baldness, perhaps from the stress of earning a living as he did. He spent his afternoons strumming on his guitar in the hotel's communal guest room. The room was badly lit with a single lamp and furnished with one stained couch and two chairs, both with uneven legs.

"Do you get tired of the songs?" I asked him from the doorway one day, essentially saying that I certainly was.

His fingers kept moving when he looked up at me. "It's a job," he said. "A routine. Beats stuffing envelopes or whatever."

"Do you have some original material?"

"A little. In places like this people just want to hear what they know."

I told him I would catch his act before I left town. He shrugged.

When I made it down to the bar later, the crowd was small. Hughie seemed to be going through the motions, wrapped up tight in memorized lines and chord structures. The Co. part of Hughie and Co. was a wiry, long-haired bassist, an awkward cowboy type who was also responsible for programming the percussion machine.

"Something to drink?" asked a waitress who was about my age.

Another accent, I thought. "Are you from Quebec?"

"Yes," she said. "You, also?"

"No. Ontario."

When she returned with my pint she told me she had followed an uncle who came west for work. I asked her what she thought of Dawson Creek. After looking around to confirm that no one was thirsty, she put her empty tray down and took a seat at the table.

"Everybody's curious about that," she said. "People pass through from Edmonton and say, 'What are you doing here? Do you want to be here?' And I know how this life can make you feel like you're missing something. But I was missing something in Montreal, also. I don't know. When I first got here I was afraid to walk down the street, it was so empty and quiet. I wondered if something was wrong, if something terrible had happened to all the people." She shrugged. "I miss my mother, and my friends, but I feel lucky to be able to try another life. I'd like to get some land of my own, maybe a few horses."

Hughie and Co. lit into the second verse of "Honky Tonk Woman." Hughie toyed with the first line: "*I laid a divorcée in Dawson Cree-eek...*" A woman sitting alone at the bar raised her glass and gave a celebratory cheer.

Weekdays, the music died at midnight. The taps got locked up, the till emptied, a cab called for the last frazzled boozehound. The town tucked itself in early. I likewise lay in bed, on top of the blanket. Cheddar cheese, a bun, and some orange juice sat on the windowsill by my feet; the exploits of Huck Finn rested open in my hand. I closed the book and threw it aside.

I wondered whether I might never call my girlfriend again. What anymore could one say? I had chosen to be alone. The drifter fable appealed. I could be a legend in my own mind, the storied and shadowy outsider whose presence sends a hurried whisper around the saloon. I wanted to be elusive as a tumbleweed, guided by external forces that bounced me across the plains, now and then—along the edge of a lake, at the base of a distant tree, on a random street corner—getting caught up for a while.

And yet loneliness seemed to be stalking me in Dawson Creek. The days here were long and silent, marked by a failure to find people who might have been able to help cure what I had to admit was boredom. Maybe I wasn't trying hard enough. I had exchanged a hundred greetings and smiles. I had slow, three-coffee breakfasts at cafés, and loitered at the public library and various donut shops. For most of one afternoon, I sat on a bench next to an elementary school's playground. I left before the children were let out (figuring I'd be cause for parental suspicion). At night, I had skulked in my bedroom at the Alaska Hotel—which seemed to have but two guests, sullen Hughie and me—and tried to write about something other than how my trip had come to resemble quotidian life.

As a transport truck squeaked loudly half a mile away, braking upon arrival in town, I had thoughts that ran together: *Yes, I'm lonely in this place. I'm also restless as hell. If I'm supposed to be a rolling stone, what am I doing sitting here like a lump?*

I got off the bed to close the window, excited by what felt like a minor revelation. I had paid for seven nights. Though tonight was only number five, I had had my fill. The bus ride south could, and would, continue tomorrow. I shut off the light and got under the blanket, feeling much better for simply having decided to move on.

6

We pulled over at a hamlet not far from the B.C.–Alberta divide. When the driver set off toward the gas bar on courier errands, a threesome of dishevelled teenagers rushed down the aisle and jumped off the bus. Dedicated smokers could complete a few worthwhile drags before the driver returned. On this occasion there was barely time to strike a match.

"Let's go, people!" the driver barked. "If you get off like that again, you'll be staying off. I told you this wasn't a break stop; I said we'd be stopping soon."

His stomach was like a bag of sand, slung heavily in his tucked shirt. The hair that remained on his head was shaved to white stubble, and he wore tough-guy mirrored glasses. Attitude and appearance must be covered in the driver's handbook: *Don't let them see your eyes. Don't let them see you smile. Don't let them off the bus.*

The three young men piled back into the bus wearing smiles, pleased with themselves for at least having tried to cheat the system. The driver stood with crossed arms, attempting to be patient.

"They can't wait twenty lousy minutes," he grumbled, dropping himself down at the controls.

Twenty minutes later he made good on his promise and we eased into the parking lot of a roadside restaurant. Some passengers made a beeline to the establishment's toilets (presumably having boycotted the bus's john), others immediately joined the procession beneath fluorescent lights to buy tacos or burgers or a milkshake. All leaped at the opportunity to stand and move.

I stood near the driver in front of the bus and eyed him surreptitiously as I did a few squats. The uniforms did have a certain military flavour. The basic ensemble was a grey blazer with navy-blue stripes near the cuffs, a dark tie, silver nametag, and generic gold collar pins somewhat reminiscent of war decorations. The material looked heavy and stiff, perhaps to facilitate sitting soldier-straight, alertness via discomfort. This particular driver also had a small leather holster for his ticket hole-puncher, highlighting what might be a frustrating impotency in his life's work.

With the assistance of a cigarette, the driver regained his calmness. His deep inhalations of chemically laced tar made obvious the addict's dilemma: it helped him to live as it helped him to die.

"It's amazing to me," he said. His sunglasses were facing straight ahead but I realized I was the only person standing nearby.

"What's that?"

"I was in the air force for twenty-five years. When you were told to do something, you did it. You didn't forget altogether or try it your own way when no one was looking."

I glanced around. His scolded charges were smoking in a cluster, facing each other with shoulders hunched. The driver coughed and spat toward the bus. "Shit like that gets me thinking about retirement," he said. "If I have any problem with this job, it's dealing with the jokers. Sometimes I'm surprised the world goes on turning."

I went to get in line for my own meal substitute. Eating on the bus was a shared experience; simply breathing meant sampling the selections around you. Roast beef sandwiches, for example, quickly permeated the available air with their B-grade meat bouquet. I was hungry, but I also wanted to be partly responsible, when we hit the road like a rolling steel burrito of bean paste and dripping cheese, for the resulting greasy funk. *We shall be united in our cheap feast!*

Through the windows I watched the driver flick away his butt and march toward the adjacent gas station. The final few people who had been served, myself included, lingered by the bus door, savouring a few more moments of openness, of bodily freedom. Then the driver was crossing the parking lot. He clapped his hands once and, waving a handful of envelopes that had been pinched under his arm, started to shepherd his flock.

"Time's up," he said. "C'mon. Let's go."

We lurched and coughed and climbed aboard.

7

Eventually, Edmonton appeared in the distance, a sudden tombstone horizon. After the North's untrampled infinite, the big city came as a shock. Here would be noise. Here would be need. I was arriving into the harried future, the wilderness of the thirsty poor and anxious many.

Edmonton was also the trip's first demonstration of a crowded bus station. Whether travellers moved slowly or fast in the terminal depended on whether they were lost or late. Those who were just waiting had a place on the long rows of hard plastic seats that faced a selection of closed, numbered doors, where each door represented several destinations. The amount of time an individual had been at the station could be measured by how far down they were slumped in the chair. The length of their trip could be measured by the thickness of the baggage wall built up beside them and around their legs.

A few taxicabs were lined up outside. "Yes, sir?" said a driver.

"No, thanks."

"What are you looking for?"

"I found it," I said, pointing ahead of me at nothing in particular. I walked out of the hot exhaust, easing myself into the city habit of haste. In minutes I was near the downtown core. I wanted to stand like a minute speck in the dimness between bank towers because bank towers seemed like a supernatural creation. I wanted to stare up at twisted clouds that appeared to offer an expression of the planet's velocity as they tore across the tops of buildings. I wanted to marvel at the action of people before the novelty faded, before the intricate mosaic became a flat mash of movement.

Edmonton's grey grid buzzed with rush-hour traffic. Stopped at a red light, I became part of a small crowd. Nearest me were a shiny young businessman, his tidy female equivalent, a man in oil-stained overalls, and an army officer. Though each was a story to guess at, each a different brand of alien, for half a minute we were a many-headed beast with a singular ambition: to cross the street. A member of a similar species was poised to move toward us from the opposite side.

No words were being exchanged. The air was loaded with the stressful silence that precedes a running race. Suddenly, a man shot out from behind me like a bullet, knocking my pack, and crossed the lanes in a few strides. *Hey, buddy. This is a team effort.* Then red became green, and the orange hand on the pedestrian signal became a white man walking. The blob started to move and divide by its parts. I wondered if we needed a coach. *Okay, everyone. Keep your elbows down and your head up. Let's get through this thing together!* Sadly, the universal mood at the end of the working day wasn't light enough for such silliness. I was the last person to reach the other side.

I stayed two nights with a friend who taught creative writing at the University of Alberta. He was also a published author, and as such was curious about my design.

"Do you have a narrative arc in mind?" he asked.

We were having a late-night beer at his kitchen table. I picked at the label on my bottle. The short answer to his question was *no*. Only in recent days had I come to realize that some kind of book-length work might be possible; surely over the course of 8,000 kilometres I would accrue enough material. But I had so far disregarded the need for narrative arc.

I mumbled to my friend about the possibility of incorporating family history. My mother's father, who had died two years earlier, was buried in Saskatoon, where he had grown up. On my father's side, meanwhile, a great-grandfather of mine had homesteaded at Yellow Grass, Saskatchewan. "I guess there could be meaning for me on the prairie," I said. My friend nodded politely, and I carried on. As for the United States, well, my mother had been born in Columbia, Missouri, when my grandfather was a university professor there. The family left before Mom turned three, but I could stop in Columbia, if for no other reason than to tell her what the city looks like today...

I wanted to shrug, shake my head, and admit with a melodramatic sigh that when it came to the question of story elements, I felt lost.

Narrative arc. My friend's words lingered as I tried to get comfortable on the pullout couch in his basement. I was trying to go with the flow, to let go of the idea of having a certain route. I was trying to trust that tomorrow would be notable, that theme would gradually emerge from reams of detail, that a winning tale would somehow just ride sidesaddle with the days and with the land.

One balmy day, I loitered for a few hours at the university. The fall term was in full bloom. Students and their baggage were spread over benches and picnic tables, and across the campus lawns. Textbooks were still shiny, notebooks unmarked. With an explosive groan, a girl collapsed near where I was lounging on a patch of grass.

"Is everything okay?"

"Oh, sure," she said. "I just had a calculus lecture from hell."

"Oh. I can't help you with that."

"I can't help myself. What are you in here for?" she said, as though I were a fellow inmate. "What are you taking?"

"I'm just visiting."

"The school, or Edmonton?"

"Both." I explained to her about my bus trip, and she taught me the mathematics of her anxiety. She was eighteen, a first-year engineering student.

"I already don't know what the hell's going on," she said. "I'll suffer through the whole year and then they'll say my marks aren't good enough for me to continue."

Her nose was pierced once, each ear several times, and her hair was dyed black and made up in many short spikes, some of which were adorned with tiny butterfly clips. The army-green denim knapsack next to her on the grass was spilling its load of class outlines. She told me she had done well in all subjects in high school. As a result, university became the sensible next step.

"Right now, though, I wonder what I'm doing here." She tore clumps from the manicured lawn as she spoke. "What's the point, you know? I'd rather be sitting at my keyboard arranging music."

"How many classes have you had so far?" I asked her.

"Calculus? Four."

"I wouldn't worry about failure quite yet."

"I know. I shouldn't," she said. She tossed away a final handful of ripped-up grass and leaned back on her elbows. "I'd *love* to be doing what you're doing. I tell myself that I'll get out someday. Visit other cities and countries, stuff like that. You going into the States, too?"

"Yeah."

"Awesome."

I understood my hesitant engineer friend's antipathy. My own post-secondary education had been inevitable. The only question was where would I go to get one, not why. And, because I had a knack for building paragraphs out of sentences, I chose journalism, a practical, will-prepare-you-for-the-world degree. During the fourth and final year, our class was given a handout called JOB$. "Look for a definition that most closely fits your individual skills," the flyer urged. I scanned the page for a suitable role. Would I find a place in the glamorous echelon of editorial, or join the invisible but rewarding research team, or perhaps enter the hand-shaking world of promotions? Even publisher was listed, perhaps for those of us keen on skipping the drudgery of entry-level work in order to lean back behind a massive oak desk and dwell on whom to fire next. As the compendium made clear, my classmates and I were about to join an industry like law or construction or post-secondary education. We were about to hop aboard a decorative, sales-driven vehicle for which words and images were the motor oil.

Okay, kids, time to survive the way we taught you to.

8

During the short ride to Red Deer, I thought about another brand of duty, the kind that was causing me to stop in that mid-sized Alberta city only because my mother's brother lived there with his wife and two kids. Not that I didn't want to see my relatives. I was fortunate to be welcomed, grateful to be in line for another serving of warmth and kindliness. But it was also true that I felt an obligation: a clear conscience wouldn't allow me to *not* pause in Red Deer.

I was apprehensive. The fact was I didn't know my uncle or his family very well. When I was eighteen and crossing Canada by train, I'd stayed with them for a couple of nights, and over the years my uncle made semi-regular trips to Ontario to see his mother, and old friends. That was the extent of our shared past. He and I couldn't claim to have more than a handful of distinct memories of each other. All we had were some of the same people in our lives, though in vastly different ways. My uncle and his clan in Red Deer were part of my extended family, a category I was beginning to see as an array of people I cared about awkwardly, those I was affectionate with at arm's length.

"Here's a towel," said my aunt after I crossed the threshold of their spacious three-level house. "I'll show you which bathroom you can use. And please help yourself to whatever's in the fridge. Treat it like home."

I suppose my appearance was that of a fellow in need of a lengthy shower and a decent meal. Here, again, was opportunity for food at the standard intervals, plus access to a full complement of bedding material after nightfall. Whether I would stay one day or three, the method was to sleep like a dead man and feed as though I was going off to war. Binge on normality.

Nineteenth-century English statutes described vagabonds as those who "wake on the night and sleep on the day, and haunt customable taverns and alehouses, and rout about; and no man wot from whence they came, nor whither they go." The pursuit of nothing in particular was still considered dishonest and dishonourable, a burden on the community. I suspected that I was indeed a layabout in my uncle's eyes. He was a doctor, a shrewd, rosy-cheeked man twice my age. Though we never specifically talked politics, I knew he was conservative. One morning, as the two of us were strolling through a farmer's market, we passed a busker playing an acoustic guitar. In the cardboard box at the man's feet was a decent pile of change.

"He's doing well," my uncle said. "And you know what? He's not paying a thin dime of it in tax."

Perhaps my uncle wondered at my own seeming disregard for professionalism. Did he think I was absent the day they handed out ambition? I had to assume. The only revealing comment was sent my way after one of my aunt's lovely meals.

"Eventually," he said, "you're going to have to, you know, *feed yourself.*"

"I know," I said.

I saw a smile but heard his teeth grinding. My aunt asked us who would like ice cream with their raspberry pie.

That night I lay in bed defending myself to myself. I had, in fact, gotten a job after graduating from journalism school. I worked for a wire service in Toronto. From behind the tinted glass of a downtown tower, I proofread bulletins that told of interest rate hikes or murder-suicides. These dispatches were sent electronically to newspapers and television stations, where a decision would be made whether someone should be sent to interview a bank executive or a grieving grandmother. I quit after eleven months (during which I had parked as much money as possible in my savings account). Then I bought a ticket and packed a bag, and one afternoon found myself looking down at the Pacific, giddy and naive on the way to Tokyo and Bangkok and a dozen havens yet virgin to my eye. My grasping at insight had begun. I was gone.

Upon my return to kindly, wealthy Canada, the murmurs got louder. *He has a journalism degree, right? Couldn't he get work at a newspaper?* I appreciated it, sort of, all that concern for my well-being. I just couldn't fill any of the roles for which I had been groomed alongside many others. I didn't want to sway public sentiment or manufacture agitation and conflict or beg preoccupied authority figures for useful quotes.

Not long after crossing the auditorium stage in an ankle-length gown to the sound of polite applause, I made a discovery: I didn't aspire to be a writer, but I aspired even less to be anything else. A few years later, however, the words I put on paper (and restaurant napkins and motel stationery) still weren't putting much food on the proverbial table. Thinking great thoughts paid poorly. Here's one that might be worth a penny: A little hunger is instructive; it gives you the perspective of the hungry.

Admittedly, this reflection comes from the pedestal of a middle class upbringing. I have never, in any entrenched way, been hungry or cold or penniless. I have never known desperate need. While a questionable use of time and money, my education was also a privilege. My parents, I believe, were similarly privileged, as were their parents. I am three generations removed from those whose days were spent keeping starvation at bay, from the families who beached themselves on a craggy shore and moved across the land with courage and as much kitchenware as they could carry.

I noticed *The Call of the Wild* by Jack London on one of my uncle's bookshelves, and wondered if he knew that London was once jailed for thirty days for being a tramp (and was likely thrilled to get three squares and a cot during his stay). I currently had no income. I was headstrong, uninterested in being a subordinate as the price of eventually having my own subordinates. Perhaps I belonged to a lost century, way back, when the natural course of things was obeyed rather than controlled, when earnings weren't the measure of a man, when property wasn't held so tightly in hand, when time was counted by curved glass and sand. Such was the tramp's philosophy.

I never engaged my uncle on these topics. Maybe, by not attempting to explain myself, by continuing to play the role of young man footloose and wistful, I only confirmed his notions. I was stuck in character as the agreeable nephew. Again, the problem, I thought, had to do with our spotty history. He hadn't been around during my formative years; none of his thoughts had shaped my own. We were never quite at ease around each other. Perhaps the problem wasn't history so much as geography—Red Deer, after all, was over 3,000 kilometres from Toronto. Even though he was my mother's brother, he could rightly be considered a *distant* relation.

In spite of the different kinds of space between us, we did have one thing in common: his name was Dave.

At the time, Dave was debating whether to put a fresh coat of stain on his house. I told him I used to paint during the summer back in high school. For three days I circled the house with brush and bucket and ladder. I did it to help out, as payment for staying there, and to demonstrate, on his terms, that I wasn't lazy, that I was a solid worker, good for something after all. Dave was impressed, and insisted on paying me for a job well done. I left Red Deer with a little hard-won respect and enough cash for at least a week's worth of greasy meals and cheap motels.

9

I lit out early for Calgary, not long after dawn. The sun was honing its glare behind horizon clouds. To my right, to the west, the mountains rose ragged out of the smooth prairie. Circular bales of hay were stacked parallel to thick stands of trees in the fields, somewhat protected from eventual wind and snow.

There was a chill on the bus. The fan blew air that was too cold for the hour, when many were still half-asleep, having hustled to the station in the near darkness, minds and stomachs grumbling. The woman across the aisle from me was partially draped in a denim jacket. Her bare legs were curled up next to her, and she was leaning against the window, brown hair mussed. She never stopped fidgeting, adjusting her position by inches, edging the butt a little this way, realigning the spine just so, and she seemed to be pushing against the glass as though to make its form more accommodating. With considerable optimism, as she was on the sunrise side, her eyes remained shut. Like others, she was lost in the effort to find rest.

The Edmonton to Calgary route had a commuter quality. It was reasonably short and efficient, and the bus emptied at either end before heading back again. There was no time to get to know fellow riders. All we had in common was a nearby destination, and, at 7:00 a.m., discomfort. The bus was an indifferent conveyance for people who were at once together and detached.

Calgary came into view from fifty kilometres away. The suburbs were our introduction to the city. Housing developments covered the outlying treeless hills like a nasty pastel moss, not a stalk of greenery shooting up anywhere to mask the growth, no claims being made to comeliness.

Dully accepting of my polluted mood, I rubbed my eyes and listened to someone cough.

A few days before I left Red Deer, my uncle had asked me whether I planned on visiting his aunt, who lived in Calgary. "I'm sure she'd appreciate you stopping in," he said. I nodded noncommittally. My great-aunt Jean was a tall and bright woman who, on the few occasions I had seen her in my life, reminded me of my grandfather. It hadn't seemed unlikely that I would drop in to say hello before I left the province, though I hadn't yet dealt with specifics. Before I knew it, my uncle had handed me the telephone, and my great-aunt's voice was rasping out of the receiver. "I'd be happy to see you," she said.

Jean lived in one of Calgary's older subdivisions, about a half-hour ride from downtown. I walked from the bus station to the nearest rail-transit stop. The Saturday morning streets were quiet; the city was sleeping in.

I got onto a car that was carrying only one other passenger. He had short though unruly hair, and he was pale and non-blinking. Because he was wearing a T-shirt with food stains, I assumed homelessness. Because he was singing, I assumed mental disrepair. My guess was he rode the rails of this closed circuit until told by authorities to become scarce and find himself a vacant parkette or a coffee shop tolerant of destitution. Sitting two benches down from me, he hummed a few quick tunes as we left the tallest buildings behind. Soon he switched from hums to whistles, serenading the morning with a variety of birdcalls. After the fifth stop, the man stood and wrapped his arms around a pole about five feet away. As I was looking out the window, staring blankly at industrial land, I sensed that he was appraising me.

"You're a visitor," he said.

"You could say that."

"I just did." He smiled and giggled. "Alberta is new territory for you. Cowboys and Indians. Cowboys and Indians."

"Cowboys and Indians?"

"And Flames and Oilers."

I nodded, locating a thread of logic. He moved to the door nearest me.

"Are you a cowboy?" he said. "Is that what you are? I'm wondering. Is that what you are?"

"I've never been asked," I said.

He looked away in silence, tapping his chin rapidly with three fingers. The train eased into the next stop.

"Or a wild horse," said the man. He was giggling when he stepped onto the platform.

I tried a few of my own birdcalls. I was alone now, left with discarded newspapers and the stale tang of to-ing and fro-ing. My eyes carried over an ocean of transit advertising. Young people like me were urged to celebrate life by drinking a certain cola or driving a certain truck to the top of a mountain. With the help of dramatic bar graphs, we were encouraged to calculate how much we would be worth when we turned fifty-five. *Will you have enough? Are you sure?* Meanwhile, elderly riders (those who resembled the worried men and women in the photos) were asked whether they knew the peace of mind that came with having a living will, or with resolving funeral arrangements ahead of time. Donations were requested from all demographics to help pay for the mystery of cancer or heart disease or poverty. Death was nothing if not popular motivation.

As I walked along hushed and leafy streets, looking for the appropriate intersection, I catalogued what I knew about my grandfather's sister. She'd grown up in Saskatoon, and eventually moved further west, raising a family in Calgary. Her husband had died six or seven years earlier. Her niece—my mother—was quite fond of her.

What did I know? Not a helluva lot.

A tall woman in a light blue flannel nightgown greeted me at the door of her one-and-a-half-story bungalow.

"Hi, Great-Aunt Jean," I said.

"That's a mouthful, isn't it?" she said. "Jean is fine. Come on in." I followed her inside. "I won't stop you from calling me great, though. Better to be called great than old."

After I set down my pack, she ushered me to the kitchen table and poured me a glass of orange juice.

"I wasn't quite ready for you," she said, tugging at her gown. "I bathe every evening and go to bed in a clean nightdress." I nodded and smiled. Soon I would remember my mother telling me that getting a pacemaker had only quickened, and darkened, Jean's sense of humour. "I want to feel fresh at the end," she said. "I want to be clean for whoever is sent to collect the body."

While waiting for the teakettle to boil, Jean thought of things I might like to know. My grandfather's first job, she said, was to keep birds away from experimental grain crops at the University of Saskatchewan. Working as a human scarecrow, he earned one dollar a day. She had also taken some physical history off the shelf for my visit. We sat over steaming mugs and flipped through black-and-white photos of relatives I'd never met; eighty-something Jean hadn't met some of them, either. She knew how she was connected, though, and therefore we knew how I was connected. Jean would say a name, and I would nod.

She set about to fix us scrambled eggs and toast. The people, places, and dates were a dizzying concoction, a brew of information from which the supporting drama, stabilizing elements such as purpose, disappointment, and desire, had long ago evaporated. I could put a finger on the grainy image of, for example, a couple on their wedding day, but how was I supposed to be moved by a world beyond living touch? Where was the sense of the individual?

I watched Jean make breakfast. (Though she wouldn't accept any help with food prep, she said she'd be happy to let me do the dishes.) She leaned into the fridge, set a square of butter on the table, shuffled to the stove, poked at the frying pan with a spatula, shuffled to the toaster, returned to the fridge for raspberry jam, forgetfulness—or gradualness—being a part of these routines. Her motions, if slow, were sure. And, probably, reassuring. Breakfast was an invitation to another day.

After we ate, Jean gave me a copy of the plot map of the cemetery in Saskatoon that would lead me to her brother's—my grandfather's—grave. He was a man I had known, his voice one I could remember. I had grown up not far from him in southern Ontario, where he had settled for the last half of his life. I thanked her, folded the map and put it in my pocket. Earlier in the trip, I had thought I might go to the cemetery because it was more or less along the way. Now I would definitely go: someone expected me to.

I thanked Jean, and walked away from her house with a full belly. I didn't even make it back to the rail-transit station before I began to feel like a fraud. Was I just pretending to be interested in the scrapbook? Had I merely made appropriate noises as she rattled off dates and names? My amenable nodding, my rap of *I see* and *oh yeah*, seemed like a wanting response. I didn't know how to react. Maybe the problem was plain indifference. Was I cruelly dismissive of family matters? I didn't think so. Would Jean and I have sat together at that kitchen table unless I had some awareness of, and concern for, whatever it was we shared? I can't say for sure.

The past did seem like a frustrating excavation. Perhaps I was a lazy digger.

A generous definition of our ancestry would include the dinosaurs, those reptilian cousins whose lives are guessed at. We shared the space but not the time. We are the bones that will litter some future landscape (our cars and trucks the rust-eaten chariots, our skyscrapers the colossal, enigmatic ruins). We are a riddle for whoever follows: Why were such idyllic, fertile plots of land used as a dumping site for the dead? And why did they bury themselves in such elaborate and worm-impermeable boxes?

For the short ride to Drumheller, the "Dinosaur Capital of the World," I had eons on my mind. As I had learned staring up from a dew-wet field at summer camp as an eight-year-old, the light of visible stars took tens or hundreds or thousands of years to get here. Some of those fireballs (said the earnest, acne-studded counsellor) actually burned out long ago. We were seeing the past, seeing life in what was dead. Whether or not my young brain understood, I was amazed. It still appealed to me, the idea of curious beings spying on the earth from stellar distances through a telescope we haven't invented: they would see the dinosaurs roaming, chewing on lush foliage and each other. In that far-out sense, they still exist, and in a similar sense, we don't, yet.

As Graceland is to Memphis and Disney World is to Orlando, the Royal Tyrrell Museum of Paleontology is to Drumheller. After wandering the grounds with swarming school groups, I talked my way into the inner sanctum as a plucky investigative journalist.

A friendly media-relations assistant ushered me to the bone laboratory and introduced me to Luke. He had a beard and longish, twisted hair that were appropriate to a worker in a fringe science like paleontology. Beneath his dust-shielding apron he was wearing a faded black T-shirt speckled with stars and planets. I suspected that he was a devoted science fiction fan who was likely a social outsider despite or because of the fact that he had a genuine interest in pursuing knowledge that would remain foreign to most of the rest of us.

He was working on specimen 941221, a plesiosaur. It had been discovered by oil prospectors working in the tar sands near Fort McMurray in northern Alberta, and had arrived at the lab as a

700-pound block of rock. Luke had been slaving over 941221 for three years, slowly coaxing the bone from the stone with scalpels and various vibrating tools.

"You learn as you go along," he said, "but basically you let the rock show you what route to take."

The reptile was still half-buried, but its outline was mostly exposed, a dark-brown form emerging from greyness, its delicate twig-like bones in stark contrast to the bland, indifferent strength of the earth that had held them together for so long.

"We don't know what colour it was, whether it was male or female, or what its habits were," said Luke. "Based on size, it was probably the equivalent of a teenager, you know, still growing and learning how to survive."

Like a dentist working on a patient who's been dead for a hundred million years, he chipped at the stone encasing the skeleton with a metal pick. Museum visitors looked in on the scientist from the other side of a Plexiglass divider. I wanted to ask Luke what it was like to be one of the planet's coroners, adding details to those textbook measurements of time that start at the start and only mention us as a way to illustrate the relative brevity of our collective walk-on part. But then a loud drill or vacuum roared to life across the room, so I yelled something like: "You guys must have a different perspective on the history of the planet!"

He smiled and shrugged.

"The planet is a puzzle, and most puzzles can be solved! But the dinosaurs came and went, and we'll do the same—that much we know for sure!"

At Luke's urging I took a stroll among the eroding hillsides on the outskirts of town, where time was catalogued by millennia. If the glaciers were melting a few minutes ago, the dinosaurs were here yesterday. Now and then I broke a chunk of mud from a knoll or kicked at a loose pillar of layered sediment. I hoped to find a random bone from one of the lost beasts, or, ideally, another tooth to go with the dirty moose molar buried in my pack. Such a discovery, in fact, was the central reason I embarked on the walk. However, after I had wandered for two hours in shallow, sun-baked valleys, the search had begun to take on a desperate quality. I decided to stop pawing at the ground and sit for a time. I inspected my grimy hands, and allowed my breathing to slow. From that point I decided to let the tooth show itself. And it soon did. It wasn't hidden, as I had been expecting, only slightly camouflaged by the crusty earth. With my thumb, I rubbed dirt from the prize before heading back to town.

Every street corner in downtown Drumheller was decorated by at least one concrete replica of a dinosaur, cracked and paint-chipped creatures that had seemingly been abandoned in favour of a new and better dinosaur. The time had come to improve, to invest, and the citizens wanted something more unique and lasting with which to reach out to the world. They constructed a fibreglass and steel monstrosity, a 90-foot, 70-ton dinosaur called Dino 2000 which had just been completed two weeks earlier. If Dino 2000 intrigued visitors, went the thinking, maybe they would stay for nine holes of golf or a night at one of the many available B & Bs.

A guy rode up on a bicycle and stopped near me on the parking lot below Dino 2000. He had dirty, shoulder-length hair and a thin moustache. He was like a thirty-year-old teenager. We stared way up into the toothy mouth of the T. Rex, where the gift shop was.

"A lot of dinosaurs around here," I said.

"Old ladies? Yeah."

I gave the man a grin. "Do you think they've gone too far?" I asked.

"I don't know," he said. "If they didn't have dinosaurs here, they wouldn't have nothing. You a tourist?"

"I guess so."

"Me and some friends used to sell fossils to tourists at the side of the road. Fifty cents apiece. We made twenty, thirty bucks some days." He spit on the ground at the base of Dino 2000. "I don't know why they gotta build a massive fake one when they got the real things at the museum."

His back tire threw a little gravel as he took off.

At a glance, Drumheller's story seemed to be that of many small towns. Its population was quietly proud and basically comfortable despite being geographically alone, a mixed crowd doing its best to consider the future collectively. In a store window I noticed a flyer soliciting leaders and supervisors for a teen club. The group, whose previous guest speakers included young ex-prostitutes and ex-motorcycle gang members, would apparently be folding if support weren't found soon.

I approached a docile clutch of kids. They were lounging on the graffiti-scarred back of a stegosaurus, poking each other and passing around a cigarette. The three girls and two boys stared at me with amused curiosity.

"You looking for nightlife?" said one dark-eyed girl.

I shrugged.

"You'd have to go to Calgary. Around here, Drumheller is it. People come here from other places, smaller places."

I told them where I had come from, mentioned Fort Nelson, Grande Prairie, Dawson Creek.

"Which way's that?" said the same girl.

"Quite a bit north of here, northwest, I guess."

"Which way's that?"

I pulled out my compass. When she leaned toward me with genuine interest, I felt a jolt of empowerment. Any lesson I had to impart might be listened to, if I was quick and succinct and entertaining with the words. I didn't have a lesson, though, nor was I sure the role of knowledgeable woodsman suited me. One of the girls giggled nervously, and the guys looked at each other with a smirk.

"My grampa has one of those," said one of the girls.

"What is it?" said another.

"A watch."

"It's a compass, actually," I said, popping the lid. "In case you're ever lost."

"Tough to get lost around here," said one of the guys.

"You have to go somewhere first, idiot," said the other, grinning as he jabbed his buddy in the arm.

"Piss off!" said the buddy, jumping to his feet to jab back.

"Looks old," said the curious girl, ignoring them. "So which way is northwest?"

I pointed to the arrow, then pointed northwest, providing a useless bearing she could safely forget.

If the day came when she wanted out of Drumheller, any direction would do.

I myself headed approximately east to Saskatoon. For a portion of the ride I was paired with a dear, deer-like old woman, silvery and fragile, who would have told anything about herself to anyone. She was on her way to the city to spend two weeks with her son and his family. The Canadian Thanksgiving weekend would be the peak of her trip.

"My husband was in the service, so we went all over," she said. "To the east coast, to the west, all the way up north." She smiled, and looked out the window, and then down at her lap. "He's passed on now, but we had many years of driving. We saw so much."

Near Cereal, Alberta, a magpie and a hawk shared a bale of hay as a place to pause and observe. They were perched a few feet apart and focused in the same direction—easterly, their backsides to the wind—like old men on a park bench who don't know each other but who have at least a fine setting in common.

"Now is the best time," she said when she heard what I was doing. She tapped her hip. "The Lord is calling. He seems to think my walking days are behind me. So there are fewer trips anymore, but at least I have fond memories of all the others."

Our conversation was cushioned by stretches of silence. What could I offer? *They say the reflex to recollect sharpens as current experience begins to lose its edge. They say memory becomes little more than a catalogue of posed smiles.* In our portion of an hour together, the woman next to me couldn't become more than a caricature, an old person, alone, remembering.

Evidence of what used to be decorated the edges of fields. Out-of-date machinery sat rusting; wooden granaries had become empty crumbling shacks. Green tractors and corrugated steel bins cast shadows over their predecessors. Railway tracks seemed ubiquitous, running in all directions, the steel scars of some previous affair of industry. A weathered caboose was being used as a roadside ice cream stand, although it was now closed for the season. And a windmill, with half its petals gone, stood frozen.

Later, an ambulance zipped silently by in the fast inside lane with siren off, spinning lights on. Inside the emergency vehicle, a paramedic was busy attaching equipment to a white-haired man. When the patient tried to sit up, the attendant put a hand on his shoulder. The bus was often a window into other windows, but opportunity could be faint for noticing was what worth noticing.

Life tended to hurry past.

IO

When I arrived in Saskatoon I contacted the Suns. Yinshe Sun lived with his wife and two children among other immigrant families in a low-rise apartment complex. My father had played host and helper when he first arrived in Canada from China a few years before, and Yinshe insisted that putting me up wouldn't be a problem.

"We have a two-bedroom apartment only," he said over the phone. "Not two different houses like your family in Ontario."

I told him when I arrived that I needed only six feet of floor space, but he insisted on relocating his mother to the couch so I could use her bed. She had come from a rural province in China to help for a few months with the family's newborn daughter. She was illiterate, had few teeth, and spoke a dialect that even her son could only partly understand. But as a mother and grandmother she knew how to handle a baby, and, with a nine-year-old boy racing around as well, the household was active.

Yinshe had just finished his doctorate in geography at the University of Saskatchewan. His language skills, however, weren't strong enough to get a teaching job. Although he was enrolled in programming courses, the uncertain future loomed menacingly. He handed me his hefty, hardcover thesis.

"What do you think now that it's all over?" I asked.

"I'm not sure," he said. "How do you say?...mixed feelings. I think maybe the PhD was a bad decision, maybe many years of wasted time. My wife and I attended the best university in China. I taught there. Here it means nothing."

"How is life in Saskatchewan?"

"It is socialism here," he said. "The rich aren't very rich, the poor aren't very poor."

His wife, Yan, looked over. "But then maybe people don't work as hard as they can," she said. "Maybe they rely on help too much."

She was busy preparing dumplings for the won ton soup we would be having for dinner along with ham and pea fried rice. A slice of late-day amber light was cutting across the room. Their basement apartment was six feet below ground level rather than ten, so while they still had to look up in order to see out, the windows were large.

Yan worked in the computer industry. She was the family's current breadwinner, although she was underemployed, and underpaid, for her skill level. Her job was an improvement, however. Back in Toronto, where they first lived upon arriving in the country, she sold cigarettes and lottery tickets to other recent immigrants.

"There's freedom here to find a better job, to get a car and house and maybe reach for another level," she said. "We want our children to join the society, not remain on the outside like us. Yinshe and I are strangers here."

At home they spoke to their son in Chinese so that he would retain some of it into adulthood, the usual slippery hope of bilingualism. They often played tapes of Chinese nursery rhymes in an attempt to plant a similar seed in their seven-month-old daughter. A beach towel was draped over the TV set to reduce the temptation of easy culture. In the evening, after his usual homework was completed, the boy spent an hour or two on his electronic keyboard. The object was to keep all parts of the brain working, all possible paths clear.

"I don't feel a part of it," said Yan when her husband left the room briefly. "When people talk sometimes I can't understand, and they just keep talking. When we watch a film or a television program, we don't always know why they laugh."

"Neither do I," I said.

She smiled. "Yes, but different."

Yinshe was showing his mother how to operate the microwave. She was cradling the baby below her chin. Both infant and grandmother looked at me and smiled. Yinshe sat down again.

"This country is 130-something years old, I think, and China is 5,000 or more. Many people here think China is a backward society. We have very old traditions. The Chinese invented paper and, hmm, for the navigation—"

"Compass?"

"Yes. Compass. China has seen much experience and change. Canada is new, a baby, and based on Europe; it is a new Europe."

After dinner Yinshe and I rode to the university on bicycles. The scene felt somewhat like an Asian moment transplanted, as if we were racing to market to fill our baskets with greens and citrus fruit, the stark difference being that hardly a soul populated the grey sidewalks of suburban Saskatoon. Cars were parked for the night and houses were warmly lit, televisions glimmering inside like controlled fires.

"I am interested," said Yinshe, veering close to me. "Often Canadian towns have Main Street. Why is it called Main Street when it is empty?"

"Good question," I said.

"Something else," he said. "I have a friend, Charles, who is also Chuck. Why is this?"

Another mystery I couldn't solve for him. Though his curiosity was real, I couldn't help being amused. I didn't tell him that I had known a few Richards in my day who were actually dicks.

We stopped on the corner of a department store parking lot to admire a statue of Gordie Howe. The moulded smile was handsome, the hockey stick poised. As legend suggested, young Gordie learned how to skate (and how to throw savage elbows) on frozen ponds outside of town. He became a big, soft-spoken man who scored a pile of goals for Detroit.

"Hero for Canada," said my Chinese friend.

I nodded, and we rode on into the bitter wind.

In the morning, Grandma was sitting cross-legged on the carpet entertaining the baby girl. Yan hurried about preparing for the workday. I sat at the kitchen table with the men, and asked their son, who had few distinct memories of China, whether he liked Canada. He was still waking up.

"Yeah," he said. He yawned, pushed a hand through porcupine hair. "It's, like, you know, good."

The boy had perfected the monosyllabic staccato of any Canadian kid who would rather be in his bedroom or outside, leaving such talk to the dull adults. Yinshe looked at his son. The boy ate his toast quickly and pushed away from the table to get ready for school.

"How do you say?… a change of soil," said Yinshe. "When you leave one place for another you must learn again how to survive— 'Where will we live? What job will I do?' But I try to not worry. I think we have a comfortable life here."

When Yinshe looked at me, his pensive eyes suggested he had just taken a peek at a decent future, permitted himself a momentary and private dream. He was busy discovering a reasonable life. I smiled. My host turned his attention to the basement windows that showed a sliver of clearing sky.

An icy wind was scratching at Saskatoon the day I went to Woodlawn Cemetery. A retired hearse, its dashboard thick with dust, its long back end full of spare tires, was parked permanently near the front gate. I consulted my map before heading down the paved roadway.

Rabbits scattered from the sound of leaves getting crunched underfoot. I joined the groundskeeper where he was kneeling next to a cracked and leaning gravestone. His four-wheel all-terrain vehicle was parked beside him, its cargo hold full of dead flowers and their accompanying cellophane.

"I guess it's just garbage eventually," I said, gesturing at the pile of dried colours.

"They come with all this wrapping so we gotta get to them or they'll blow away," he said. He was wearing a white balaclava to deflect the cold autumn wind. I could see only his eyes and mouth as he spoke. "Some of the plastic ones we leave." He paused, and I had the impression he'd never really discussed his job before. "The real ones don't last forever."

My grandfather's plot was sunk in the short grass on the outside of a circular lane.

Walter Robertson Elliot. 1910-1998.

While standing there, I remembered first the misery of my grandfather's final months. His mind was strong, his body an uncooperative shambles. He lay in a tilted bed and waited. Eighty-eight years of the sound and imagery of experience quickly became a burden. He was, I believe, more than ready to die.

At his funeral, I had provided a eulogy on behalf of the grandchildren. (As a would-be writer, I was the go-to guy whenever a few suitable words were needed. I had scratched a poem together for my sister's wedding, and came up with something appropriately witty when one of my brothers got hitched.) I couldn't remember the memorial speech, other than the fact I kept it generous and brief.

I remembered how, back in Calgary, my great-aunt had been a stark reminder of my grandfather: the long body and wrinkled gaze, the sharp intellect. That recognition was real, infused with significance, and as such was something I could carry away. Perhaps an idea was all I carried away from my visit with Jean: how mutual genes are there for the witnessing. As I shuffled my feet, I realized how Walter and I (and my mother, too) had similarly crooked toes. If history repeated itself, I'd probably someday need a version of the orthopedic shoes that allowed him to walk through his last decades comfortably.

I cleared my throat, and looked around as if someone might be watching to make sure I was being suitably respectful. The groundskeeper had driven away; I was alone. Perhaps because I was cold, seemingly callous questions came to mind: How long was long enough to stand here in the flesh, shadowing a stone? Would a quarter of an hour suffice? Or did sincerity not kick in until the thirtieth solemn minute?

I trusted Walter would grin at my gallows sarcasm. My jittery pacing, however, may have irritated him. He might have asked me: "Aren't you in the middle of an unusual pilgrimage of some kind? Well, then, why don't you get on with it?"

A grey feather was stuck in the ground inches from Walter's modest monument. I accepted it as a gift and pinned it behind the band of my broad hat. On my way back to the front gate, about twenty Canadian geese flew low overhead, a gaggle of honkers that formed a V pointing south.

II

On the way to the home of the Steers in Yellow Grass, a one-grain-elevator village about an hour and a half south of Regina, the world appeared as two wide, severe smears, sea blue above and muddy yellow below. The fact one of my ancestors had lived here for many years didn't make the landscape any less extraordinary to my eyes.

The Steers were a fourth-generation farming family who lived a mile from town. My great-grandfather Cameron's original farm was kitty-corner to Blaine Steer's; our ancestors had been friends. I called from Saskatoon and he said to stop by if I was going that way. His invitation established my direction.

"You didn't pick the prettiest time of year to pass through," said Blaine, greeting me on the driveway. "She's drab-looking, all scraped and brown; but that's fall for you. I wouldn't want to live without seasons."

The day was scheduled for taking the last of the grain off the fields, but he said I could join him on one of the combines. I dropped my pack inside the farmhouse. Minutes later I was riding next to Blaine, gliding over the land in a gas-powered razor worth 130 grand.

"It took a lifetime to get to here," he said. "Last century, 160 acres could support a family, easily, now survival would be tough with less than ten times that much."

The Steers had recently received the Century Farm Award in recognition for their perseverance against the odds. In Blaine's estimation, Yellow Grass was a living relic.

"The small towns are the meat of this province and they're rotting. People hang on as long as they can, but eventually they have to give up. Costs are high and you don't get much for the grain. The old guys can make it work because they've been around for so long—they're not paying for the land anymore."

He had thinning blond hair and a wind-rosy complexion. He was attentive and steady as a truck driver navigating his first thousand miles of freeway. Harvest may be labour-intensive, but I imagined it had certain steady rhythms, which provided for a guy and his thoughts.

"I really like this piece of land," said Blaine. He released the controls and swung his arms out in front of his body, with palms down, like a slow-motion breaststroke. Or as if he was showing the soft outline of a lady, but horizontally. "A beautiful, gentle slope runs right across here. When I'm out here I realize the land isn't so flat after all." He looked over to see if I agreed.

"Yeah," I said, keeping my dubious thoughts to myself.

Flat did seem like the best and only word. In fact, as we rumbled along at three miles per hour biting another even strip out of the wheat, the world was reduced to a matter of length and width; we were the cursor moving across a vast two-dimensional screen. The fields, though, were an extension of Blaine's body; he knew the lay of entire swaths of land like his own skin: the smooth patches and gentle curves, the problem areas and sore spots.

His farm was in a flyway zone where geese often passed overhead, either heading out to feed or heading back to a nearby marsh for the night. They were crossing then: a conveyor belt of polka dots on the sunset sky, a coded message of curved checkmarks. Blaine set the combine to idle while he checked something in the blades. I jumped to the ground and realized that the progression of birds was loud, too, a laughing chorus of horns. Blaine came over beside me and we looked up, believers curious what the gods might scatter next for our consideration.

"For all that the prairie appears as nothing, it's a busy place," he said. "These fields are active. White-tailed deer just hide and wait as if we won't mow the patch they're standing in; you always hit a few rabbits at night; hawks are slow to take off, and owls, one time when I was swathing lentils I came up to this owl. It was sitting there like a carving, and it went right under the machine. I looked back, and it was perched on the line behind me. I have no clue how it wasn't killed."

Earlier that week the spinning jaws of the combine had chewed a skunk to pieces, and the smell was still strong. We climbed back in and the machine forged ahead, creating a blizzard of dust from the ground up. The grain torn from the stalks was quickly filling the bin behind us, a small mountain of amber pellets. Blaine called his son, who was home from college for Thanksgiving, to bring over a truck and take the load. The truck arrived and was driven alongside as the combine spit out the grain.

Blaine looked at me. "It's a little bonus to have Carter here. Another pair of hands, you know. Not stopping is worth ten or fifteen acres in a day, which is an hour or so, which, over a week, is an entire day saved."

It was a life lived as though the day had twenty-six hours, or twenty-seven. Time seemed *too* valuable. The combine hit a slight ridge and the machine's mouth became gummed up with soil. I jumped down to help with the unclogging, yanking out clumps of straw and dirt, my arms extended between the circular blades. Back inside the combine Blaine let out a sigh of frustration.

"Harvest is a tense time of year," he said. "One lost hour becomes three, a lost day becomes four or five. Every minute is a mad push because you know the frost is coming. Weekends don't exist and I often don't know what day it is. If I went to church I'd just sit there and think about what wasn't getting done."

On our way back to the house at midnight, I noticed a faint glow to the north, a slightly sparkling blush. Blaine said the light from Regina travelled into view over the earth's curvature. In a separate direction I saw what looked like another city, much nearer, and seemingly on fire: it was a field where flax had been harvested; the straw was getting burned in piles to facilitate easier seeding the next year. As my eyes adjusted away from the headlights, I realized these fires were everywhere, orange alien eyes watching over the dark land.

My hunger and fatigue—hours of jouncing in a combine can come to feel like a workout—fed a little late night pondering. We sat down to a spaghetti dinner rich with the significance of origin. Suddenly, pasta wasn't born in plastic, or grown along patterned aisles at the superstore. Suddenly, the buns and butter and Black Forest cake ` and tall glass of milk placed in front of me involved a cooperative climate and hard labour and favourable market conditions.

I was offered their daughter's former bedroom for the night. She worked a nearby ranch with her husband; their own daughter, still an infant, was known to perch beside Mom or Dad in the combine. The silence was thick. I kicked loose the floral sheet, and let my uncovered feet hang off the end of the short bed. My mind went to work, resisting full slumber, straining as though to hear that which made no sound: the softening of seed coats, the bend of ancient grasses, the weightless revolution of moons.

I slept shallowly, and woke the next morning with a wheeze. Dust from the dry land, dander from hobo cats.

Downstairs, Blaine was paging through a book of Yellow Grass's history, which included the original grid-division of land. Every square had a name, a pattern that never changed, except that the squares got bigger and the number of names shrank.

"That's Wilkinson's now," he said. "That's Dalton's, that's where your family's place was."

He left to phone the neighbour who had, for the past forty years, worked what had been my family's land. I could hear part of his conversation from the other room. "You haven't found chunks of concrete anywhere, holes of any kind?"

He came back in. "No traces at all, apparently," he said.

My father had been in touch with Blaine over the years, exchanging historical notes and evidence. In the first year my great-grandfather broke five acres and cropped none; the next year he broke another ten acres and cropped the first five. He had four oxen, one cow, a twelve-by-sixteen house, and a stable, each frame building valued at fifty dollars. Eventually he married and the couple had three children. Black-and-white photographs bared the truth of a fragile existence. The house, the people, and the collection of animals stand humbly in a row, loose fixtures for the wind to focus its steady breath on.

In one of the photos, a number of people were clustered together near the house, perhaps on a day of collective reaping. Blaine pointed his finger at one of the men.

"That's my great-grandfather, I believe," he said. "Funny. If your family had stayed, our life might be your life today. You might be living across the tracks."

Though Blaine was right, and though I was indebted to him for a generous and noteworthy day, I was already thinking about my proximity to the border, thinking ahead to America. We shook hands goodbye and I returned to the Yellow Grass depot to catch the daily that went south to Weyburn and Estevan.

12

On the bus between Weyburn and Estevan, I lent an ear to a recovering alcoholic.

"I've been sober for two and a half years," he said long before I knew his name. "I drank for decades; hard to believe. You look at the world differently sober. Actually, looking at the world at all became a new thing."

Mr. Wiseman—I didn't quite believe that was his name until he gave me his business card—had two Thermoses with him, coffee and iced tea. He drank the coffee first, four cups of black decaf in steady succession. His nerves were permanently frayed, as if forever expecting the old medicine. Between each cup he chewed down a couple of breath mints. In fact, something was always entering his mouth, and always some body part was in motion. His knees bounced up and down like pistons firing, and sometimes his free hand joined in, tapping softly with the rhythm.

"You know, ninety-eight per cent of crime is related somehow to alcohol or drug use," he said. "And only ten per cent of those attempting to recover actually do."

I wondered if the social science somehow contributed to his self-concept. "Are you succeeding?" I asked.

"Sure, sure. I suppose I have her beat. But she never goes away; she never dies."

Her? She? He discussed the demon drink like it was a woman who kept breaking his heart. My hour with Mr. Wiseman became an intimate confessional. I realized again how a bus trip could be a single session of mobile psychotherapy, a brief, forced intimacy. He said he was having trouble keeping a steady weight, and had shot from 135 pounds to 180 and back again over the last year.

"Here," he said, handing me a bag of pretzels. "I can't take any more of these."

Mr. Wiseman was a frail thing, with pale, bony legs jutting from oversized shorts and dark arm veins like wires that were the only thing keeping his hands attached: a frenetic marionette at the mercy of some invisible puppet master.

"Drinkers don't eat, you know," he said. "They drink."

They also talked. The facts kept coming: his wife was a painter; they lived "in the country up north"; he didn't have a driver's licence; he used to repair truck transmissions until he tried to lift something he shouldn't have and found himself dealing with constant pain.

Although I was, as usual, intrigued by the tale being told, I found myself fighting mild resentment. At a glance, I thought I had seen empty seats further back in the bus, enough of them that anyone who wanted to could sit alone. Why were Mr. Wiseman and I together? At the moment, I wanted some space. I wanted to be contemplative, brood for a while, gaze mindfully through the filmy glass that offered a partial reflection of my bearded mug.

For several kilometres at a time the air near the road was dense with grain dust, the outside world temporarily out of focus. The blurriness never lasted long. We pulled away from these ground clouds like a missile groaning toward some target not yet visible. I had never seen so far. I had never seen so little. The occasional farmsteads that drew my eyes from the horizon were like ghost ships anchored on pale shores.

Ever since leaving Yellow Grass, a practical concern had been weighing on my mind. Neither Greyhound nor its local subsidiary serviced the forty kilometres of highway between Estevan and the American border. I would have to improvise, depart from strategy. Perhaps there was a local shuttle bus company that could get me there, though that seemed unlikely, and paying for a cab—if there was one—didn't appeal to me. While the idea of hitchhiking wasn't especially alluring, it seemed to be the only available option. Would I get there? How long would it take?

I was also dealing with a more abstract uncertainty. The United States loomed. Its foreignness was a concern. What had I learned in school about the Dakotas? Nothing. Who did I know in Iowa? No one. In recent weeks, a bed at night had been easy to come by. I had knocked on friendly doors, employed connections of various strengths. Familiarity fed me well. All of that which I'd had to lean on was now behind me. Excited as I was to get an extended glimpse of several states, not without fear was I advancing toward the adventure ahead.

Perhaps—and just in time—I was becoming an embodiment of the myth of what it was to be Canadian: surrounded by uncluttered, incomprehensible vastness, I was looking inward. Noticing that his wrinkle-wrapped eyes were trained on an imaginary point across the land, I supposed Mr. Wiseman was doing the same.

"I don't remember a whole heckuva lot from the drinking years," he said. "That's the troubling thing. When you get a certain ways down the line you got to have something of value behind you."

I nodded, and crunched into one of his pretzels.

"Oh well," he said. "I think I figured myself out before it was too late."

For me, it still felt early. Maybe the pieces of identity are scattered at the beginning, right from the Big Bang of birth, and life is taken up with the meticulous assembly of found truths. Maybe a theory could be strung together with scraps lifted from the actions and aspirations of people around you.

As Mr. Wiseman began to drum a simple beat on his thighs, I looked out the window. Estevan, I trusted, was only minutes away.

Walking south out of town at 9:00 a.m. on the holiday Monday of Canada's Thanksgiving weekend, I was motel-rested and hopeful. I tried to tell myself that covering the remaining forty kilometres to the border was an entirely realistic goal. At 2:00 in the afternoon, however, having not received a single sympathetic nibble, it seemed somewhat closer to impossible.

To hitchhike is to pray, an act of freeway faith. Rather than kneeling with palms pressed together, the believer alternately stands and squats with one thumb out. Despite discouraging scientific truths (vehicles pass, rain falls, the sun sets) the devout must not abandon their ideas. Hoping for a miracle is permissible and even recommended.

I idled for a time slightly beyond the town limits, my pack plunked down in the short grass like a boulder, doubt slowly forcing belief from my overheated brain. When a pickup truck actually stopped to pick me up, I thought it might be a mirage conjured by woe and weariness.

"God tells me when to stop," the driver said. "He told me you were okay."

"In that case, thank you and thank God," I said, and was glad to hear him laugh.

I leaned back and closed my eyes, relieved to feel movement again. My saviour's name was Miles. His truck felt like a cozy, condensed rumpus room: the bench covered with a plaid comforter like a battered, beloved chesterfield, the mud-framed windshield like an oak-encased television set, a small colour print of the Virgin Mary taped to the dash like a faded but cherished hand-me-down painting. Miles was a manual labourer in Estevan, although he lived in nearby Bienfait because "smaller is cheaper." He was divorced ("she got the money, I got the kids"), and he had a few of his own roaming stories that he didn't have the time to tell. But, Miles advised me, "best that you do this now before you suddenly have reasons not to."

We had spent nine minutes and nine kilometres together when he pulled over at a fork in the road, one prong leading to Bienfait, the other to the still-elusive border. I shouldered my pack and thanked him.

"Listen," he said. "If you haven't made it there by dark, watch yourself. We've had some rabid coyotes around recently."

He drove off. I waved, and then shielded my eyes to survey the sun, which was providing an unseasonably warm afternoon but was passing across the sky at its usual rapid rate. After quickly measuring the hours left until dusk (about three) against the kilometres separating me from the border (about thirty), I pictured myself staggering into customs in the middle of the night, hoping they somehow wouldn't notice my frothing mouth and frantic, poisoned eyes. Deciding that walking beat waiting, I marched down the highway at a healthy clip.

Stepping over the remains of flattened snakes and the spectacular damage done to the odd raccoon and fox, I felt like a potential casualty, surveying the scars of an asphalt battleground. But I also saw giant grasshoppers crossing the quiet road safely in five bounds, and thick, furry caterpillars inching along in my direction or the other, safely parallel to the white line. Plus there was a bird. I stopped walking to watch closely as it approached from the west. A hawk? No, too large. An eagle? Perhaps. It circled above me as though suggesting I take a longer and better look. I saw the round tan face, the dark and wide eyes: an owl. I remembered Blaine's story about the owl in the field of lentils that somehow managed to remain unharmed by the swathing machine. The bird's wide wings flapped once like hands waving, before it proceeded over the fields. I was in good company. I would arrive safely, eventually.

Now and then I turned to face a focused trucker as he rumbled past or an elderly couple in a big car heading for Lawrence or Lincoln, nothing but home, home on their minds. About ninety minutes later, another driver was pulled by instinct onto the shoulder of the road. I ran up behind the brown truck and tossed my pack in next to the crumpled corpse of a large off-white bird. A dog was barking inside the cab.

Bill lived in the country a few kilometres from North Portal. He operated a hotdog cart in Estevan. He said he'd be happy to get me to my destination, and we were preciously close when he slowed his truck onto the shoulder again.

"Saw some pheasants," he said. "Come on. You can help flush them out."

He grabbed his gun from behind the seat where his spaniel Rusty was frantically pacing, anxious to play a role.

"Not this time, boy."

Then, as Bill marched in his camouflage gear with long soldier-strides through the weedy ditch, I jogged beside the road, fiddling with my instant camera, knowing that it wouldn't adequately capture the instant. Suddenly, three of the birds took flight from the ditch in different directions. Bill aimed and fired. He missed, and smiled up at me.

"Bet you didn't know that not everything shot at gets killed," he said. "Especially when I'm holding the gun."

We watched the pheasants wing their way toward another temporarily safe patch of land down the highway. What Bill really hoped to locate in his scope was a turkey.

"If you can find one, they're way better than what the stores are selling," he said. "Wild beats tame every time."

I asked about the dead bird in the back of his truck.

"It's a sandhill crane. Leftovers," he said, smiling. "They're strange ones, you know. When you see them in the sky they're always just circling and circling, but somehow they make it all the way to Texas. I guess they like taking their time, would rather get there slowly."

At the border, he stopped the truck across from the duty-free shop. We shook hands through the open window. Rusty was in his lap, tongue wagging.

"I hope they don't tear your bag apart," Bill said, and I could tell he was only half-joking. "So where's home for you when you're not doing this?"

I might have said something about finding home in many places, how it was a certain state of mind rather than a certain city in a state (or province or territory); or I could have tried to explain that home is wherever we often feel thankful, wherever we are always welcome. *Home is where the start is*, I could have said. But I answered in the usual way: "Most recently I've been living in a small town in Ontario. It's on Lake Huron, called Kincardine."

He looked at me with an odd grin. "Okay. I'll tell ya what. Whenever you make it back there, go into the Sunset restaurant and say 'Hi' to the blonde waitress for me. Her name's Pam. She's my sister."

"Really?" I said. My family often ate at the Sunset on Saturday mornings.

"Yeah," he said. "One of those small world things, I guess."

"Yeah," I said.

We both fell silent. Rusty's excited breathing was the only sound. Bill was lightly nodding his head. The silence stretched too long (twelve or fifteen seconds), an acknowledgement that he wasn't ready to drive off into the evening, and I wasn't ready to enter the U.S. Who knew if his thinking was as maudlin as my own: *There's cohesion here! This blue planet can be read like a blueprint!* I couldn't help toying with the word preordained, wondering at the kindhearted trickery of the universe. *Of course* it was this very man who picked me up and delivered me precisely where I cared to go. *Of course* it was likely his sister Pam who had often served me an all-day breakfast in a rural town two provinces over. Call "those small world things" mundane, or call them momentous. Don't call them coincidence. Coincidence is too cleanly an explaining away, a sterile term for the enchantment of the everyday.

And yet, whether or not magic was at play, what was there to do but smile, shrug, and walk on? I shifted my weight from one foot to the other, fighting the delirium of a long day on the highway. "Pam is map spelled backwards," I said.

"That's true, too," said Bill.

He navigated a U-turn, and waved. I watched until his truck was but a floating brown dot. Then I turned and took aim at U.S. Customs. Whether or not fate was clearly on side, the future seemed like a fine idea.

13

I fully expected the boys at U.S. Customs to be mistrusting. My dirty, multi-pocketed backpack must have seemed a tricky vessel of illicit freight. I wore a wide-brimmed hat that threw shade over my weary eyes, and I had the overgrown facial and head hair that suggests to many an inexcusable disdain for social norms. And I had just crossed the quiet prairie border between North Portal, Saskatchewan (pop. 80) and Portal, North Dakota (pop. 100) on foot, reason enough to be presumed guilty of something.

Besides, I imagined that doubt and suspicion were a key part of job advice posted on the office wall: *Appear dour and be wary at all times while on duty. Although you may be permissive and good-natured at home, don't bring a vulnerable countenance to the workplace. Here, you are decisive and all-powerful—act that way. Free passage into our nation is not a simple right for the hopeful folks idling beneath your steely gaze. It is a great privilege.*

A blond, closely cropped deputy sheriff type came outside and waited for me near the door. With about five paces separating us, I stopped walking to allow for the showdown of first impressions. He crossed his arms and squinted—the practised look of stern judgment—and quickly fired the usual bullet: "Where are you from?" This I considered a multiple-choice question. "Canada," I said, obviously and unspecifically.

"Okay, but where are you coming from?"

"Well, I started up in Alaska, the Yukon, actually. I'm taking the bus to Florida, so Portal is about the halfway point, I guess."

Likely story, his face seemed to say. And apparently I had provided too much information too fast. The handsome young officer was on the verge of irritation.

"What I need to know is where you came from today."

"Oh. Estevan, Saskatchewan."

He paused. "So where's the bus?"

His malicious half-smirk indicated that he had made a joke. Since his job involved stopping every morsel of infrequent traffic, regular bus service was something he would know about. That particular doorway to the United States (the Portal portal) is mainly used by long-haul transport trucks and local families with friends on the opposite side, plus the occasional stray RVer who thinks he's found a handy shortcut to either Chicago or Calgary. The officer was also vaguely amused, I thought, because I was so clearly a baggage-search candidate and he had time to kill.

"I had to hitchhike," I said.

He nodded as though that matched his guess. "Step inside, please."

Inside, as he began dissecting my bloated corpse of a backpack, I pulled a few sweat-wrinkled traveller's cheques from one pocket and some American cash from another, modest proof that I could afford to loiter for a while in his expansive, expensive country. Meanwhile, he had found my kitchen-in-a-plastic-bag: a jug of orange juice, a half-loaf of bread, a banana, some raisins, peanut butter and a jackknife.

"Breakfast?" he said, grinning across the room at his co-worker, an older, pot-bellied man who offered no reaction, resolved to remain unimpressed with life. Any element of surprise had vanished from his job long ago. The wall beside him was plastered with missing and/or wanted persons flyers: sons abducted by fathers, or daughters who simply disappeared. The grainy black-and-white photos seemed to capture people when they were looking lost—wide-eyed and caught off guard—and now represented the paper-thin hopes of someone stuck searching.

The young officer's inspection descended past my sleeping bag to my slim wardrobe: three Ts, a sweater, a pair of jeans, a hooded raincoat. When he got deep enough to regretfully finger two pairs of crusty socks, lifting them out and releasing them quickly like dying fish, he speeded things up considerably. From the pack's lid came my toiletries satchel, and from the side pockets a tape player and two novels.

While placing *The Call Of The Wild* and *The Adventures of Huckleberry Finn* on the counter, the officer whispered the titles to himself, perhaps wondering what those particular books indicated about the person who has chosen to read them. Eventually, with the various pieces of my moveable life laid out like crime-scene evidence, he took a step back.

"Awright, I think that'll do. Do you always live like this?"

"You get used to it," I said. I looked down at the backpack, now resting empty, deflated. "Holds everything I need."

He wasn't quite satisfied. "But where do you live? I mean, where will you go after Florida?"

"Oh, probably back to Ontario for a while. That's where I grew up. Most of my family is still there."

He fell silent.

While repacking, I reversed the interrogation. "How's life in Portal?"

"I don't live here, thank God," he said.

"You live somewhere bigger?"

"Anywhere's bigger."

"Somewhere twice this size—two hundred people rather than one hundred?"

"Exactly," he said, not seeming to mind the little poke. He was quiet and aloof, a cautious talker, though again I wondered whether the reticence was genuine. Border authority was often a robot act, efficient and humourless. My desire as usual was to glimpse the individual beneath, know something of his true self. I looked out the glass door and across two lanes of summer-bleached asphalt. A lone eighteen-wheeler was pulled over on the shoulder, its hazard lights flashing. Beyond the truck lay anonymous fields, scruffy plain that gave way to more scruffy plain.

"So," I ventured. "Have you guys busted any refugee-smuggling operations recently?"

"Not much crime at this crossing," he said. "It's not as exciting a job as you might think."

He followed my gaze out to the long grasses. He pursed his lips, and appeared to be chewing on the inside of his cheek. Presumably he was turning over thoughts, about the prairie, how its endlessness can seem a strange restraint, or about shift's end, a lawn chair and grilled meat and something cold to drink. I waited.

"I guess I do get to talk to all sorts of people, from different places doing different things," he said. "Folks from all over, going every which way. I suppose I like that part."

He made this admission as if for the first time. While handing over my passport and cash he allowed himself to smile, perhaps having decided where to file me in his mental cabinet of characters who requested permission to enter.

"Just sign this and you can head for Florida."

I scribbled along the bottom of a piece of paper. I fancied I was promising to be a thoughtful nomad, to create few disturbances and to leave and shut the door behind me after discovering what I came to discover. The customs officer walked me outside and, with a crunching handshake, said, "Good luck the rest of the way."

The slightest of bonds had been forged: he was on my side now (and, quite literally, I was on his). As though I was the trusty horse and the backpack my dusty, sunburned rider, the southbound trot began once again.

I advanced only another hundred metres, however, as far as the Americana Motel, where I decided to bed down for the night. I was ready for a rest, and had adequate reason to pause. Six weeks earlier I had been passing through the Yukon. In another six weeks or so I would be in Florida. Besides which, begging for rides all day along a quiet belt of prairie highway had been a gruelling exercise.

After showering, I stretched out on a mattress of thinly cushioned metal springs. Eventually I propped myself up with pillows and watched the road through the open front window. The early October night was cooling quickly as the sun dropped away and the clear sky surrendered its blues. About one vehicle passed by every minute. I closed my eyes and could hear a steady breeze rustling the trees behind the motel, and a dog barking madly in the distance. Then the telephone rang, startling me.

My father's voice crackled loudly out of the plastic receiver. "You were easy to find," he said.

I had stopped at the Americana because, unsurprisingly, it was the only motel in town. And Dad is a proud sleuth. Although I hadn't talked to him in over a week, he knew where, and approximately when, I planned on crossing the border. Among other curiosities, he wanted to make sure I hadn't been detained and roughed up by antisocial Customs thugs.

"If they mistreated you, we could send in the Mounties," he joked. "I could make a call right now."

"I don't doubt that," I said.

"So, are you getting what you need?"

"What I need?" I knew what he meant: was the road trip justified; was I gleaning enough wisdom from the winos and waitresses across the land? What of singular value had I observed?

I related my hitchhiking drama for Dad, in particular the heartening conclusion that starred a man named Bill, and, in peripheral roles, Bill's sister Pam and Kincardine's Sunset restaurant.

"Really?" he said. But his next comment suggested he wasn't surprised: "These things happen here."

By "things," I assumed he meant interconnections and neat overlappings. And "here" was simply here, the whole of a sprawling planet, the small world, this ball of infinite threads.

As we talked, a small camper van pulled in to the parking lot and idled in front of the room next to mine. The driver was a middle-aged man, and, as far as I could tell, he was alone. He unfolded a map over the steering wheel. He was lost, perhaps, or merely indecisive. Out of habit, my eyes fell to the van's licence plate, an instant locator of origin. *Ontario. Yours to discover.* I felt an urge to wave from the window, or even go out and say hello.

"You're starting to see the big picture?" Dad was saying.

"I guess. Maybe the big picture is a combination of smaller pictures."

"There you go," he said. "Better jot that down."

As we arrived at our goodbyes, which included my promise to call sometime soon, the Ontarian reversed out of his spot and drove back to the road. I hung up the phone and put on my shoes again. It was time to track down an American beer, an American burger, and a few talkative Americans. The man in the van hadn't yet exited the parking lot; he was signalling but not turning, even though both directions were free of traffic. As I was halfway toward him, he finally disappeared to the south, rolling past the motel's end.

Whenever you leave, and wherever you go, I thought, home finds a way to follow.

14

Two days after being graciously accepted into the United States, I found myself still immobile at the border. In order to connect with Greyhound's American route I had to get to Minot, 150 kilometres away. My motel room in Portal was cramped, dark, and stale, and the prospect of spending a third night there didn't please me. I imagined that a procession of various living things had arrived inside the door only to collapse and die. Additionally, I could no longer stand the stuttered groan of transport trucks gearing up or down, nor the jukebox at the town saloon that was stuck on the vain anguish of cigarette cowboys.

Such dread was inspiring. After unsuccessfully pleading with truck drivers and off-duty customs officers for a ride, I loitered by the gas station and waited for an appropriate target. Before long, an older couple in an Alberta-plated car pulled up. The husband slowly unfolded from the vehicle and started decoding the pump instructions. He was vulnerable prey. I walked over, removing my hat in case he thought it was the proper thing for a stranger to do in such circumstances. My hands were held out at the sides with palms faced forward like those of someone approaching a scared animal.

"Excuse me," I said. "I don't suppose I could get a lift down to Minot with you folks?"

He looked up. Took me in toe-to-head. "Sorry," he said. "We don't do that."

I forged ahead past the stern denial. "The problem is that the bus doesn't pass through here," I said. "I'm a friendly Canadian boy. You have nothing to worry about."

"We don't know that," he said.

I felt guilty playing the Canadian card, but I was desperate to escape border limbo, anxious to plunge headlong into, well, other obscure places in North Dakota. I played another card.

"I'm a freelance writer," I said. "A journalist. I'm crossing the continent collecting stories."

He was silent in thought. I could almost hear the ice breaking.

"He's a journalist," he said to his wife through the open passenger-side window. I stepped back to let them deliberate privately. After a moment I was given the green light to throw my bag in the back seat. As I did so the husband went to talk with the driver of another Alberta-plated car at the adjacent pump.

"Maybe if you could stay close behind us for a while," said my new host.

"Does he have a gun or something?" the second driver asked with a smile.

I leaned over to participate in the joke: "Canadians aren't allowed to have guns."

The second driver turned to me. "They haven't taken mine away yet."

Portal was only a few miles behind us when suspicion started to fade. The woman, Frieda, told me she had done some newspaper writing in her day, which I realized had probably won me passage. I didn't tell her how I was seeking a valid detour around run-of-the-mill journalism. Examining my reticence would not have smoothed the welcome. In their eyes (despite my shaggy facade) I had a calling. I trusted Frieda was pleased enough to think I was someone else who fooled with words, a colleague of sorts. Her husband, Rob, also wasn't worrying about the legitimacy of the new cargo. He leaned over the steering wheel as we sped between farms.

"How fast can we go now?"

"Sixty, I think," said Frieda.

"How fast is sixty? I can't read the dial: these miles numbers are too small."

Frieda turned to get a better look at me. "We have a son who has a beard like that."

I told her I would probably let it grow until I got home, as a measure of time gone.

"He likes his, too," she said. She smiled and looked back to the road.

The sun warmed the car, and made my eyelids heavy. I settled in, drowsily watched prairie towns go by—Flaxton, Bowbells, Kenmare, Carpio. Soon—though I hoped not too soon, because I was enjoying the cozy novelty of the ride—we would get to Minot, where a minibus awaited to take me to Rugby, the geographical centre of North America. Dad had circled it on the road map back in August. Suddenly, I was almost there.

15

I was racing toward the geographical centre of North America in the widow's two-door turbo, going sixty, sixty-five, levelling out at seventy when the road beneath me got to feeling soft and a dirt cloud lifted behind that might have encouraged a time-killing cop to give chase. The borrowed Buick had some kick. I was supposed to leave Rugby later that day, take a minibus to the station in Grand Forks, where a Greyhound pass for the U.S. was waiting for me. But now I was in the leatherette captain's chair, possessing freedom and automatic glory, the ability to floor it. In fuel-injected, climate-controlled comfort, I could pull up dust all the way to Texas, maybe not stop until I got to a town called Canadian that sits in the north of that state. I had seen it on the map. Perhaps I would be received kindly in Canadian. And who knows, the widow may have liked me enough to not report the car stolen. She may have accepted her confusion as to why her gentle boarder would run off and do such a thing. I could write to her from Monterrey; rather than extend an apology, I could invite her to leave her life behind and join me. Someone on the radio began to sing a sad song about sad songs. I had to laugh.

I eased off the gas and coasted, scanning the cropland that swooned now and again at the demand of creek valleys. I was looking for a certain field, in the middle of which would be a slough, in the middle of which would be a pole. The pole, hammered into the pond's muddy bottom by government surveyors seventy years earlier, marked the centre of North America. As the nearest town of notable size, Rugby got to take the credit. A tall and proud stone cairn on the highway was festooned with the flags of Canada, the United States and Mexico.

"The centre thing is kinda neat," the Chamber of Commerce representative told me when I arrived in town. "People will stop in any weather to take a picture of the rocks."

Dubious or not, the geographical centre distinction was why I had come, the reason I'd decided to place Rugby on the path. In time and space it would be an approximate halfway point, the magnetic heart of the ride. Rugby would be a detail to which surrounding details could be attached (which made for a reasonable definition of centre).

A slough came into view on the driver's side. I pulled over and got out of the widow's car, groaning to myself. I was still coping with a hangover: dry-mouth, a stunning headache, and—worst of all for a guy intending to document his life—the misfortune of partial memory loss. Beer and whiskey made for a harsh rehashing. When I closed my eyes and stretched, I saw stars (not, of course, like those of the previous night, spilling down the sky away from the aura of a full moon). Blood pounded past my ears. I turned west to face the wind that eerily made little noise as it had little to rub against. Breathed deeply through my nose. All I had to do was find the start and work forward again slowly.

Rugby, North Dakota.

Booze, guns, haunted houses.

The widow.

Rugby's Chamber of Commerce, which operated jointly as a tourist information centre, had its offices adjacent to the gas bar where the bus from Minot dropped me off. It was almost 5:00, and I was beginning to wonder about finding a place to spend the night. The amiable town official winced when I asked about accommodation: every motel in town was booked solid. Many out-of-state hunters were in the area shooting at beast and bird, he said, and Minot was hosting a large Scandinavian heritage festival. My only option was to stay with one of the locals who took in boarders at affordable rates.

"Great," I said. When he went to his office to make a few calls on my behalf, I fingered a rack of postcards, feeling blessed. I was about to be invited inside. My first night after leaving the no-man's land that was the border, I had walked into the possibility of staying at someone's house. Who would I meet? How would that person spend his or her days? What unguarded admissions might be made in my presence?

The Chamber rep returned to the main room wearing a smile. He had found a woman with space to let. Although two custom combiners from Oklahoma were using her basement, another spare bedroom was still available. As I lifted my backpack, he suggested I relax. She was on her way over to pick me up.

A woman I had known for twenty minutes was laying bare the facts of her life. She was a physical therapist at the Heart of America Medical Center. She made seven dollars an hour.

"The American Way," she said. "I earn too much to qualify for help but not enough to live."

I was sitting at her kitchen table. She was scurrying around preparing dinner for us. Two sizable steaks were bleeding on the barbecue, a few potatoes buzzing in the microwave. Once she was also sitting, she looked over at me and released a little air. Then I received the sticky truth around which the rest of her life made a patterned web, the thing she thought I had to know about her before I knew anything else that really mattered.

"My husband died seven years ago," he said. "He had a massive heart attack. He was working at the hospital, standing at the doors to the ER when it happened. He was thirty-six."

That, as they say, was that. *Widow* was just another statistic, after all: height, weight, marital status. Her eyes were brown, her hair dirty blonde. She had a son about to graduate from the local high school, and a daughter in her early twenties who lived in Bismarck, a city two hours south. The older family portraits that were sprinkled around the house featured four agreeable faces, the more recent ones only three.

A miniature collie nosed into my hand below the table, seeking either affection or undercooked meat. As we ate, the widow asked about my sudden appearance in her town.

"What do you think you'll find here?" she said.

When I said I wasn't sure, she smiled, and suggested we go for a walk around town after dinner.

"You'll see all there is to see," she said. "It's not much."

The day was easing toward its end when we started out. There was no machine racket on her side street, and all the cars I could see were parked. The peace was pervasive, as though the entire community had changed into something more comfortable and was sipping a well-deserved after-work drink.

We tried to wander residentially to minimize our encounters with traffic, although the freeway was a steady din easily heard if you tuned in. We passed the water tower. Rugby's was in the inverted beaker category of water towers, with sleek curves and a crowning bulb, recently painted orange. We passed a mobile home dealership. Affordable and portable aluminum cubes were set in a row like wedding cakes. Slight differences in colour and design made for the appearance of choice. *You can tow it, stow it, or throw it onto some far-removed plot of land. Whether you have many neighbors or none, moving it around is half the fun!*

The widow grew up in Balta, sixteen miles from Rugby, sixteen miles from the highway.

"I walked back there in the summer," she said. "I always wanted to walk back, maybe just to say that I did. I was amazed, listening to the wind, watching for movement across the fields. I felt like I had never been down that road before, even though that road is the one I know best. I was in the middle of nowhere for the first time."

She pointed out a house that was choking on its Halloween decorations. Cardboard ghosts, inflatable witches, streamers and signs and bushes filled with tiny purple lights. The owner seemingly couldn't wait until Christmas to spread some high-wattage cheer and prop up the local merchants.

Or not.

"She probably stole it all," said the widow in hushed tones. "Rugby's shoplifter. She's not allowed in any of the stores anymore. They turn her around at the door."

We walked on.

"See that house on the corner back there?" she said, thumbing over her shoulder.

I stopped to look.

"We can keep walking," she said. "I'll tell you what happened."

The year before, two teenagers were drunk and racing a car around the neighbourhood. Eventually, they lost control and drove into a house, killing an old star-crossed man as he was watching football.

"His body was thrown into the next room," she said.

The driver from that night was later sentenced to two years in prison. His slightly older accomplice had bought the beer. The widow's daughter had been joyriding with the guys earlier that evening. She started to get worried and told them to take her home.

"She saved her life getting out of that car," said the widow. "You never know what might have happened to you. Only what did."

We were several houses along. I turned around and took another look. The evidence, of course, was long gone; the house repaired, grass grown over the skid marks. The home was dark inside, the driveway empty. Cursed, haunted, permanently stained with an ugly moment. The next buyer couldn't know the story.

"People went nuts about it," she said. "But kids are no worse now than when I was young. Back then there was one cop in town. We always knew which side he was on; we did what we wanted on the other side."

Back at home the widow announced her need for a hot shower. She handed me a stack of photos to help pass my time alone. She wanted to share one of her trips with the traveller. The previous spring, her son's high school class had gone to New York City and Washington, D.C., and she went along as an escort. I flipped through the usual evidence of statues and war memorials, but there were also a few armies of pigeons featured and pictures of traffic with the phalanx of yellow taxicabs: the city as captured by a complete stranger to it.

The widow came back to the living room in robe and pajamas, combing her wet hair. "New York was something," she said. "When you look up you can hardly see the sky. People move down the sidewalk in a big blob, avoiding eye contact with each other. And the blob splits in two for the homeless; you see them just in time not to trip over them."

Lying back in a recliner, she turned on the television and started flipping vacantly. She stopped at a trivia game show.

The widow tilted her head my way, eyebrows raised. "What would you do with a million bucks?" she asked.

"I'm not sure."

"I'd make sure my kids were set for life," she said. "That's what I'd do first. Put some away, let them have it as they need it. And I'd probably move out of Rugby. Get a nice place in Bismarck, maybe. But I don't know. Life might just look better somewhere else until I got there. Then I might wonder why I left."

The TV contestant was knocked from the game, her total winnings a measly sixty-four grand. Over the next few minutes the widow did some mental accounting, weighed assets against debts, calculated a quick bottom line. She told me that her salary hadn't really changed in fifteen years.

"It goes up two per cent a year," she said, "but the health insurance increase is three or four. I'm actually moving backwards." She was wearing a tight grin. "And I can tell you that it doesn't pay to be a widow."

"No?"

"The funeral took most of what we had. The money we got in the cards paid for the stone; nothing was left after that. We had never bothered with life insurance."

Seven years past trauma, she could be candid. Misery didn't appear to have a foothold. Her husband's death, however, was a continuing source of agitation in her affairs. The widow's mother-in-law was upset that she'd started dating nine months after the young man's heart attack; she was still sending letters of disapproval and reproach. One of these letters had arrived that day; the widow took the unfolded pages into her lap. Her lips moved slightly as she read, as if she wanted to read it aloud, had to hear it to believe it.

"She said to me, 'He would have waited at least two or three years to try and find someone else.' I can't understand her. She wants to take her sadness out on me. What does she want me to do? Maybe she'd feel better if she knew I haven't found anyone else—but then, she does know. She knows everything she wants to know. We work on different floors in the same building."

"Is Rugby too small sometimes?"

"Sometimes. There's nowhere to run and hide. But then if disaster hits, people are aware and they're concerned. When my husband died I realized all these people knew who I was. The town closed around me."

She yawned. Checked her wristwatch. She was expecting her son home any minute. He worked part-time as a hired hand at someone's farm, and he had a grand vision.

"He wants his own land, his own machines, the whole package," she said. "I told him, 'If you want to, fine, but it's gonna be your load to bear.' I can't worry about him all the time." She glanced up at the wall clock to get a second opinion on the hour. "I wonder why he's not home yet."

The widow curled up her legs and started chewing a fingernail. A few minutes later the boy called.

"He's hungry," she said, putting the phone down. "He's always hungry."

She went to the kitchen and stuck her head in the fridge. I could see her feet below the open door, pale bony ankles in soft slippers. I grabbed the remote control and hit mute.

"A farmer's life offers no guarantees," I said.

She looked into the living room at me, a square of ground beef in hand. "Except constant struggle," she said. She dumped the pink meat into a pot, and started stabbing at it with a wooden spatula. "I guess life offers no guarantees for any of us."

I sat there in quiet conjecture. If her own expectations had been cut down like ready shoots of grain, she would be hesitant to nurse those of others, put her fragile faith in the clumsy hands of someone else's imagined future. Hers hadn't even been a dream, I supposed, merely a comfortable, livable arrangement. All she cared about were the happy consequences of work and love. Now, as she stood over the stove, rotating her shoulders, she was just following the mother's code: keep your head up as proof-of-poise to the little ones; keep your disillusionment to yourself, your weaknesses out of sight.

The prodigal son arrived home. He was wide-eyed but looked worn out, dressed in mud-speckled farm fatigues. He flopped onto the couch to wait for his food. I introduced myself.

"You wanna buy a used truck?" he said.

The idea appealed to me momentarily—my own vehicle, my own schedule—but I had gone too far now not to finish the ride according to original design.

The widow's son had two vehicles: the pickup truck, and a near-classic Dodge Charger that his dad had bought for them to take apart and rebuild, slowly and together. He had vowed never to sell the Charger. It sat in the yard next to the garage surrounded by gas canisters, tires, and other spare parts.

The widow handed her son a plate of chili, and he handed her the yearbook he'd gotten at school that day. She sat down and started flipping through it excitedly.

"What's the big deal?" he said.

"You're graduating."

"Looks like you're the one graduating."

Eventually they both went off to bed and I was left with a sleeping dog and the tireless television. The widow was herself somewhat keen on decorating for October 31st: witch stickers on the windows, paper leaves on the walls, pumpkin buckets and stuffed creatures placed about, plus, in the front yard, cloth ghosts, corn stalks, and hay bales. Most notable, perhaps, was a wide-eyed, curly-haired doll in a rocking chair wearing a Happy Halloween bib. The chair and doll were prominently positioned in the living room. I suspected that she was a permanent fixture and that a different bib was provided for every seasonal celebration.

I went to the spare room, and prepared to turn in. Maybe the widow could see aloneness approaching fast and wanted to keep her home filled with the imagery of active lives being lived. Maybe she was attempting to be normal and maintain order despite a growing suspicion that normality and orderliness were illusory, hopeful creations of a mind seeking merely to be at ease. I left my clothes in a pile next to the queen-sized bed, slipped under the puffy floral duvet, and lowered my head onto a sweet-smelling pink pillow. I couldn't help wondering if this had once been the conjugal bed, moved downstairs for guests because the widow could no longer bear to use it. Couldn't resist the sane reasoning of another's story. Couldn't resist the lyrical reduction, the temptation to be conclusive. I slept long and hard.

Most of the basic services were in view from Rugby's main intersection: four bars, two banks, a gas station, a drugstore, a bowling alley with neon ball and pin. A row of concrete grain elevators made a formidable wall to the north, the water tower a proud totem to the south. I turned in place. Reassurance had me surrounded. The rhythm of life was steady, unconscious. No surprises, no confusion. The bells of several churches competed to declare the portions of every day; one or two cars were always idling outside the post office as mail was sent or collected; 2nd Street ("Main Street") was never busy and never barren; sidewalk conversations were brief but mandatory.

—How's life today?—Depends what we're comparing it to.—
Yep.—How's your day?—Good, good, you know.—Will we be seeing
you Saturday?—Oh, sure. We'll be there.

Familiarity was assumed. People nodded or gave a two-finger
wave over the steering wheel before they realized they didn't know
you and looked back as they wondered just who you were, anyway. It
came to my attention, however, that all of those friendly wavers
probably did know me, that is, they knew *of* me: where and with whom
I was living while in their inconspicuous town.

One afternoon I received a phone call at the widow's house from
the reporter at *The Pierce County Tribune*, Rugby's weekly newspaper.
The reporter was an acquaintance of the widow's; in the Canadian
wanderer, she smelled a story. Would I answer a few questions? Okay,
I said. Would I mind if they took a picture? Sort of, but go ahead.

I decided to let irony have its way with me.

On my fourth and last night in town, I met up with the widow
and two of her co-workers for hamburgers at a pool hall. Over beef
and beer a plan was hatched to drive into the country and visit a few
abandoned farmhouses.

The widow and I shared the back seat of a monstrous four-door
pickup truck. Although the scene might have included such things as
chewing tobacco and bad grammar, my companions were well-
groomed young professionals, merely using the night to erase the day.
The two men up front were wearing decent button-down shirts and
ironed khaki slacks. Bud was driving. Colt, riding shotgun, had a
shotgun in his lap.

In a minute and a half the town was shrinking behind us. Colt
said Rugby was too big for his tastes. He lived about thirty miles north,
not far from Canada, away from the call of neighbours.

"I like feeling like I'm alone in the world," he said. "Just me and
the land and all the little animals. And my gun."

The others laughed. On a roadside pond, five swans landed in
near-unison like a team of fighter jets.

"Terrible eating," said Colt. "Too tough. But they're a beautiful bird."

For a few miles the road was bordered by marsh. The calm pools of water were dirty mirrors in the fading daylight. Several muskrats were busy with the duties of dusk.

"Look at all those buggers," said Colt. "Let me take a shot."

He jumped out of the stopped truck and from ten yards put a shell into one of the muskrats. The shiny animal was cut cleanly into two pieces. One half turned in the air, splashing back down a few feet from the other half. Another muskrat swam over, foolishly curious. Colt quickly took aim. He struck again, but not quite dead-on. What remained of the animal started swimming in a tight circle as though only the legs on one side were still attached and functioning.

"You didn't finish him," said Bud.

"Leave him," said the widow.

I wondered if Colt felt a need to entertain the visitor, if his firearm antics were a demonstration of life as usual or something just a touch more outrageous. Though I don't believe any of us wanted the night to be typical. The full moon was a pale orange eye watching from the horizon, diseased and Cyclopean, adding the demand of expectation. And it was rising quickly, the lens trying to get focused.

"Isn't this romantic?" said the widow.

Some part of her must have thought so; another part wished that it were true. Between her and me sat three brown paper bags: beer, wine, and whiskey. All four of us were drinking, and quickly, and the camaraderie developed with ease. Colt leaned forward to get a better look at the moon.

"A great night to get drunk and put a few holes in stop signs," he said.

Bud laughed and turned up the volume on his chosen rock and roll. I could hear him singing along faintly when no one else was talking. Eventually we arrived at one of the old farms. The house and barn were monolithic shadows at the end of a long driveway. Then the truck's headlights illuminated the grey, neglected home. People like us had broken the windows, but all curtains were undamaged and drawn, as though privacy still mattered. Colt pushed open the front door with the barrel of his gun.

"Anybody home?" he said, grinning.

Our two flashlights criss-crossed and lit the emptiness eerily; we were like the first detectives arriving at the scene of a multiple homicide. Vacated wasp mud-hives were in corners and on lamps, bird nests on bookshelves. On the kitchen counter were a few clues to the story: a tube of denture glue, a knitted sweater, a teakettle; relics of some stalled existence. Perhaps the old folks died, the last of the family line, and there was no one to step in behind them. Or, more likely, bankruptcy: slow failure and forced migration.

I walked into an end room and panned around with a light, an invitation to ghouls. When I got back, the widow and Bud were crouched in the shadowy dust thumbing through a box of books. Colt wasn't with them. Then we heard the sound of a rifle shot from upstairs. And another. The bullets rang off something outside. I wondered if our man Colt was in some kind of dreamy standoff with corrupt local authorities.

"Crazy bastard," said Bud. "How the hell can he see what he's shooting at?"

"The moonlight," said Colt, entering the room.

Satisfied that enough dust had been disturbed, we got back in the truck and drove away. The next couple of hours were spent rumbling around the countryside, staying within a ten-mile radius of town, stopping only for one of us to urinate. From every distance and angle, Rugby was a cluster of speckled white light like the last seconds in the short life of a sparkler. As in Saskatchewan, some of the field stubble was on fire. Wind-assisted, the ditch grass burned quickly in a straight line. In some places the road was a wall of dark smoke. We whooped as this fog swallowed the truck, hoping for a surprise on the other side.

One of the times we pulled over, Colt set an empty beer bottle about ten yards down the road, loaded the gun and handed it to me. *Give this*

Canadian guy something to write home about. He told me how to line the target up with the metal nipple on the end of the barrel. I shut one eye but I think both were closed when the gun went off. My ears screamed. Faintly, I could hear laughter. I looked down the road. The bottle had disappeared entirely.

"Good job, man!" said Colt.

Hands slapped my back. I had lost a virginity of sorts. After that, we seemed to go faster and the dated music seemed to get louder. We hit an occasional washed-out gully, dropping in, bouncing out. Once, while bracing herself, the widow's hand fell on mine. She smiled. The liquor between us was gone. In front of me, Colt had his rifle angled out the open window like a naked flagpole, the long barrel rap-rapping against the doorframe.

At some non-specific moment, my able memory shut down. The hours were getting lost. I worried about what I would forget, and what was long forgotten. I mourned how time gets pissed away, even when you steer a course to places like Rugby, North Dakota, just to create lasting and worthwhile points of remembrance. Just to be out of range of your own ordinary.

Time gets pissed away.

Time *got* pissed away.

Time was. Time was. Time was the crooked pattern cut by piss into a dusty road.

I was dizzy drunk. Rudderless. Temporary.

I stared closely at several sloughs. I also scanned, sometimes from the driver's seat without getting out of the car, what looked like ponds and marshes and bogs. My search for the pole at the geographical centre of North America began to feel hopeless. Perhaps the slough it was planted in was having a high water season, and was covering the top of the pole. Or the pole had toppled. Or the tourist info guy had given me faulty directions. I decided I wouldn't find it.

At least I had an easy journey back to town, with air conditioning and country tunes and a drinking sickness that would soon shrivel to the point where I would be only thankful the previous night had happened. Every notable moment would return apace. I remembered the target practice, for example, and felt relief I hadn't swung the barrel at my toes, or at Colt's kneecaps.

Nor was the moon forgettable. After returning the smoking gun to its owner, I had walked behind the truck, away from the glaring headlights, and looked up. At the top of the sky the moon was as small and bright as it would get; my eyes had to adjust before they could see the crater tattoos and how the circle seemed to be cut perfectly out of blackness. The world around us was lit evenly as if by an unshaded bulb hanging from the ceiling in an empty room. *Like in a dungeon*, thought my addled brain, and I realized that, even with so much available space in every direction, a person could feel anxious and trapped, caught in a corner of the world that had no corners.

What I couldn't recall was exactly when our delight petered out; when one of us decided for all of us that enough was enough. The widow and I had apparently been delivered home safely. Something else happened, though, in the blur before passing out. What was it? After we got home, the widow and I snacked on something in the kitchen, and then we sat in her living room for a while. I parked beside her on the couch, I believe, and I started to massage her shoulders. And, after, did we hug? Kiss? She looked at me from the stairs leading up to her room.

—Should we?

—I'm not sure.

No question I woke alone.

The dirt road ended at the highway. I turned east, hummed over the final paved stretch toward Rugby. The widow was at work, and I had a bus to catch. We wouldn't see each other again. I would shower, pack up, and scribble a note to leave on the kitchen table. Already I was thinking about what to say before *thank-you*.

16

Bus stations can be sorry sites. They're never very far from the damaged heart of a metropolis. Pigeons pick at gum-dirty sidewalks next to vacant brick buildings charred by exhaust. Strays and the downtrodden, if they want out of town, have no choice but to stick around. People, many of them alone, stare at their shoes, snap through magazines, or chew a stubborn nail. The prevailing aura is one of abandonment. Bus stations are holding tanks for the dispossessed.

Such, anyway, was my impression in Minneapolis one October dawn. Perhaps weariness painted the world grey. Those arriving from elsewhere dispersed quickly via public transit or on foot, while those waiting to leave (like bent, bleary-faced me) took up all the space and defined the place. Dazed newcomers flowed in, dragging a heavy duffel bag behind them or hauling a stuffed pillowcase over their shoulder or pushing a cardboard box rigorously bound with duct tape. They were weighed down in limbo.

Was I in fact waiting to leave? If so, I hadn't yet decided where to go.

I hadn't slept especially well on the overnighter from Grand Forks, though the real problem was not quality of rest but quantity. I had just dozed off when the bus pulled into Fargo at 1:00 a.m. There, however, I had to switch buses, and the next bus to Minnesota didn't leave for an hour. Thus began a sweep of minutes during which I could neither sleep nor read nor add more than a few grunted words to any conversation.

Fortunately, I didn't need to say much to befriend a certain ex-con. In Fargo we had sat, with one empty spot between us, on the row of chairs adjacent to the Minneapolis gate, waiting for the same boarding call. He had been handed his freedom that day. "I was six months in county," he said. "Got out this morning."

I nodded.

"I gotta get to Aurora, Illinois, by tomorrow," he said. "My wife's pregnant and they're inducing labour in the morning. I think I can make it there. I gotta make it there. Think I can make it there?"

"I don't know," I said. I managed to ask him if the authorities had rushed his release so he could be there for the birth.

He shrugged. "I don't think so. I'm just lucky, I guess."

Many would say the ex-con was committing a heinous fashion crime. His blond hair was short on top, long and curly down the back. His blue jeans were tucked into cowboy boots, and he was wearing a red-striped shirt inside a too-small nylon jacket. He had either been given another prisoner's civvies by accident or he dressed himself hurriedly at the Salvation Army (which, as he told me, was where he got the necessary funds for the bus ticket).

The bus to Minneapolis was half-full. I used the extra room to advantage, bending one or sometimes both knees across the empty seat while praying for rest. Sitting across the aisle from me, the ex-con was attentive and frazzled, as though he had just exited a dream into an existence equally strange. He looked toward the front when the bus slowed or stopped—readjusting to traffic rhythms and checking to see if there was a serious hold-up he should worry about. Once we hit the steady speed and promise of I-94 he seemed to relax a little, was better able to focus on fewer things. His eyes drank in the scenery of night. The freeway lingo—billboards, restaurants, appealing neon vacancies—was enough to keep him awake. Plus he had a lady, and liberty, to think about.

In the morning we met again. The ex-con approached me where I sat, deliberating my next move. He dropped an athletic bag at my feet.

"Could you watch my stuff?" he said.

"Sure."

At the bus station, faith is based on proximity. The person next to you is the one you trust most. Among the first facts you know about him is where he's going, and how long he still has to wait. If he's similarly burdened by luggage you can be reasonably sure that he'll still be there when you return from the cafeteria or washroom. And then maybe you can return the favour. Maybe you even have the same destination.

The ex-con trundled off, his weary lope and his nervous gaze calls for compassion. If sudden freedom looked like this (a roomful of squirmy, malnourished, claustrophobic humans), what did it feel like? I watched him ask somebody a question, and they pointed him in the direction he was already going. I couldn't help thinking that his life was probably a series of minor mistakes occasionally intensified by crummy luck. In a gang of petty burglars he would be the naive dupe who followed through on unwise orders, innocent despite his guilt.

I realized I hadn't found out what he did to be robbed of six months of life, and I knew somehow that I wouldn't ask. About this blip I experienced shoddy reporter's remorse, although not much. The man's crime was one more small detail. Just as easily, I could have disregarded the fact he was about to be a father. Another truth: the world at that moment wasn't astonishing. I resented the pressure I put on myself of looking in order to see something critical. I lacked the strength to gather lessons. Hell, I was off duty. On a sunny weekday morning in Minnesota, with Minneapolis still working out from under the shadows of St. Paul, I simply could not care about the fullness of a story, whether my own or that of the kindest stranger.

When the ex-con returned, I asked him to guard my pack. It was my turn to stroll, speculate on the day. Find a future. I went to the arrivals/departures board, and had a quick study. The list was an inviting cornucopia of cities; a menu of places, with the times next to them like prices. *I might start with a serving of Des Moines, Iowa, and then, let's see, I guess I'll try the Kansas City, please.*

A plump Russian woman came up next to me as I perused this registry. She was wearing an ankle-length overcoat and had a full set of metal teeth. She wasn't afraid to smile, though, or ask for help.

"*Nyet*, Buffalo," she said. "*Nyet*, Cleveland. *Nyet*, Chicago."

She was either telling me where she didn't want to go, or suggesting places I should avoid. We took turns tapping on city names. Spoken words were only serving to confuse. I eventually discerned that she was going to Indianapolis, and that she had two hours to wait. I pointed at the clock, and drew small circles with an index finger to indicate time passing. She nodded, put one palm on her forehead, and closed her eyes, the universal symbol for exhaustion still to come.

As for me, I voted to keep going, and I would indeed resume the feast in Iowa. How did I decide? Simple: the next bus leaving the station was a bus to Des Moines. In thirty minutes I'd be on another cruiser, slumped on the left side, getting drowsy under the sun, with a sweater as blanket spread over my upper body, and the engine's white noise as a lullaby.

17

For the feeblest of reasons I decided to tumble from the bus in Ames, Iowa. Though Des Moines wasn't much further down the interstate, I thought a smaller place would be more quickly and easily navigable. Plus, Iowa's state university was in Ames, and while in America I wanted to—or thought I should—visit at least one of its vine-hung copyhouses of fruitful futures. The bus pulled in; I hopped off: what the hell. The destination would have to explain itself.

Ames had greeted me strangely. In bold black letters on a white strip across the side of an office building, I saw written: JESUS IS YOU. As we approached the depot, the message was quickly behind me, lost to the flow of traffic.

Shortly thereafter I was in a fancy high-ceilinged foyer at Iowa State selecting from a roster of cultural experiences. A bulletin board was plastered with a choice of distractions. My eyes passed over that which hinted at philanthropy or charity (honourable but dull), and anything to do with sports or film (predictable and potentially dull). The Chi Alpha Christian Fellowship, however, seemed to leap off the board. The group was meeting later that day. Further down, my eyes stopped on the Chi Alpha flyer itself. "We're about authentic spirituality and serious fun. Come. Free your mind." Reminding myself of the day's original omen, I made plans to observe a little group religion.

The gathering convened in a room where normally a buttoned-up academic would hold forth on economic theory. A lectern sat front and centre, and an aisle ran down the middle of rows ten seats across: the church look improvised. I arrived fashionably late and settled into a back corner seat.

All eyes faced forward; a three-member band was between songs. An electric guitarist in a tropical shirt was standing next to the drummer, who flicked his wrists over a four-piece drum set. The singer was putting the next song on an overhead projector so the crowd could join in. She was youthful and energetic and when my eyes came to her she was smiling my way. I was disquieted, as if she knew me without having been introduced. When she returned to the duties at hand the room took a collective breath.

Let there be praise
Let there be joy in your hearts
Sing to the Lord, give him glory…

The music was cheap and tinny and too loud for the small room, but apparently worship doesn't have to sound good to feel good. Some of the twenty parishioners had their palms together, while others kept their hands free to wipe away tears or sweat. Some were standing. Everyone's head was rocking at least a little. At different times many eyes were closed (unless their owners needed help with the lyrics), and many arms would fly straight up and start shaking as if palsied. The effects were passionate and trance-like, a reaction I had never seen to a drug I had never tasted. A handful of shy near-converts lingered near the door behind me, humming and mumbling softly.

Few people other than myself were looking directly at the singer, but she centred the room's attention. She had brown curly hair. One of her hands remained on her flat belly, while the other floated at her side; her hips swayed gently, as if a slow easy current was carrying her along. I didn't know if I was captivated by her spirit or drawn to her physicality, but her mind had clearly taken over her body.

A warm-down period of personal contribution followed the set of songs. Everyone spoke softly and simultaneously, a chorus of murmurs: "Dear Lord, we are nothing next to you, we give you the honour that only you deserve. You are the Almighty. We hardly deserve to look up to you. We serve you, Lord. Thank-you, Lord. You have redeemed my soul from the pit of emptiness. Hallelujah."

Then the featured speaker (who, it was said, "had unhooked teens from drugs with the help of the Jesus factor") was introduced. He was thirty-something, with glasses and a dark, impeccably trimmed moustache. He knew his audience well, the trusting and pliable.

"I would like you to see God for who He is, and see yourself for who you are," he said. "Who's read Ecclesiastes? You know: 'Everything is meaningless under the sun.' Man, is that ever depressing. Because if it's all meaningless, what are we doing here tonight?"

A good question, and one that nagged at me as the evening threatened to grow long. His words entered my brain in brief spurts, the point obscured by the protracted path he took to get there.

"The pain of discipline must outweigh the pleasure of sin," he said. "My father was a Pentecostal preacher, and, let me tell you, we had a healthy fear of him. If he said he was going to punish us, he would deliver. But sometimes the Lord leads us with pain, like a mule or horse with bit and bridle. Before I found God I was in a shop thinking about stealing a candy bar, but I didn't. Somehow I knew that even though the owner wouldn't catch me, God would take a candy bar's-worth of hide out of me."

Eventually, grateful applause told me it was over. A green plastic bowl was passed around.

"We'd like to bless tonight's speaker for his time," said the group leader. "You can make cheques out to me and I'll make sure he gets them."

I loitered at the back of the room where bags of potato chips and pitchers of ice water were set out to encourage post-event mingling. No one was afraid to approach me, the stranger. Many inquisitive eyes were set upon me briefly. The singer didn't wait long to walk over.

"I've been wondering about you," she said.

"I was just passing through Iowa," I said.

My line didn't shock or confuse her. "It's so cool that you just showed up."

The singer was a student of God and psychology. On a thin chain, a gold cross, small but radiant, rested in the V of open buttons at the top of her silver blouse. She took my hand. "Let me introduce you to a few people."

At least half of the attendees were exchange students from Indonesia and Malaysia, two of whom were the worship band instrumentalists. I asked them what they thought of Iowa.

"Corn over here, corn over there."

"Corn everywhere."

We laughed. Throughout the chit-chat I felt the singer's eyes on me, debating, decision-making. One of the ex-addicts walked over. He was attending these gatherings by court order. He laid his story at my feet, as though full disclosure to people he didn't know was part of recovery.

"I was on meth mostly," he said. "For two weeks I didn't sleep for even five minutes. Then these guys got a hold of me. At first I was like 'get outta my face' but eventually I opened myself up to God. When the preacher blessed me it was like a lightning bolt; I just dropped on my ass. And that was it."

As the group thinned, the singer and I were left alone. I said I would be in town another day or two at most. She scribbled her name and number on a Chi Alpha flyer.

"I don't know if you have plans tonight," she said. "But if you want I could show you around or whatever."

I grinned like a fool as I waited for her to go to her dorm room and change. From whence had come my sudden charm? Because I had shaken every hand? Returned every smile? Or did she just want to help a young outsider who bore some resemblance to a errant shepherd? Whatever the reason, I determined that the phone numbers you should be given are the ones you didn't have to ask for.

The singer was a different creature entirely when she returned. Her hair was tied up through the back of a ball cap that was pulled down tight. She was wearing faded blue jeans and a hooded ISU sweater zipped to the top. She looked dowdy, like a student locked away cramming for finals; makeup and finesse for worship, homely anonymity for the world.

I was curious if her appearance was meant to dissuade me from considerations of conquest. She need not have worried. We were playing the same game differently. She didn't believe in sex before marriage and I didn't believe in marriage, respective positions that precluded a brief, torrid affair. In fact, as we walked toward one of the student restaurants near campus, she said she had dumped a guy she loved because he wasn't going to be a dedicated Christian.

"He was a humanist," she said. "A really good person. But ultimately our partnership was doomed. The union wouldn't have been blessed. In a way, my feelings were irrelevant; better that I let him go."

We took an available table in the absolute centre of a small but crowded room. The place was candlelit and filled with soft music, a step above the student pub.

"I want this to be on me," said the singer.

"That's not necessary."

"I want to. You're a traveller, you probably don't have much, or never treat yourself. Don't think of it as charity, just as a treat. It's just a meal."

"Okay," I said. "If you insist."

"I insist. And go crazy, choose anything," she said, scanning the menu. "Do you want something to drink? You don't have to not drink because of me."

The singer said in general she was a teetotaller although she was known to share an extremely occasional bottle of wine with her roommate. Her hushed tone and the way she leaned a few inches closer to me suggested the detail was something she thought should be kept secret from the world I wasn't a part of: she could tell me anything.

She seemed pleased when I succumbed and ordered a glass of wine to go with my pasta. When the food arrived she intertwined her fingers and smiled at me.

"I just have to do something first: 'God is great. God is good. Let us thank him for our food. By his hands we all are fed. Give us, Lord, our daily bread. In Jesus' name, Amen.' I just love that. I think it's so cool."

She plunged a fork into her fried noodles. Her nails were painted silver and on one wrist she wore a bracelet of coloured beads with H-O-P-E threaded into the middle.

"My mother would freak out if she knew I was doing this," she said. "Hanging around with a guy I barely know."

"Would she think this was a date?"

"Dinner for two? Definitely."

Her parents lived in a suburb of Des Moines, although her father, a truck driver, was often away from home. The good news was that she'd once been allowed to accompany him on a trip to the west coast; the bad news was the way in which he tried to make up for lost parenting time.

"He would be gone for weeks, and when he came back he would discipline me. The consequences of social behaviour aren't easy for a kid to understand; eventually I realized that he did what he did for the good of our family."

The consequences of social behaviour? Her psych classes and the religion had bred a peculiar hybrid. "You were punished for things you did when he was gone," I said.

"Yeah," she said. "The penalties would accumulate."

"I'm sure you were basically a good kid, though."

"I guess, because of my parents. For always reminding me what bad was."

The singer was always covering the angles, rushing to what seemed most appropriate, some right and ready reaction. When she told me she said the Lord's Prayer every night before bed, I pictured her as a six-year-old kneeling in teddy-bear pajamas, her eyes clamped shut with wishes. The image also fit her as a sixteen-year-old, and it may yet when she hits twenty-six.

"With God I'm in a safe place," she said. "I'm always at home, somehow. Being with God is it for me, that's my place. And I'm definitely with God when I'm singing. It's been that way forever. I used to sing into my hairbrush when I was a kid."

I couldn't help being reminded of my ex-girlfriend. The two women had a fundamental vibrancy in common. I had admired my ex's excitable nature, her ability to inject worth into the everyday. She laughed louder than me, cried longer, cared more deeply. Her emotions were hung out unashamedly for all to see, like undergarments on a clothesline. One way or another, she always reacted. She *felt* life more than I did.

Although hesitant to recognize the fact, I missed her. While we may not have known each other as well as we needed to in order for the pairing to last, we knew each other like nobody else. This sentiment hit me acutely as I looked into the candlelit face of someone I didn't know from Eve.

After the plates were cleared, the singer and I decided to change the setting and headed back to campus to wander a little. The evening's pep rally was letting out, and we became two small fish caught in a river of revellers. The event was called Yell Like Hell, ear and throat preparation for the big game that weekend against Texas A&M. The Cyclones didn't have her support. "I'm proud to say I've never been to a game."

A red convertible brimming with blondes went past us in a shiny blur. The singer was quick with her disdain for sorority sisters. "I just can't talk to them," she said. "They're like candy: very sweet, but you can't take much of it without feeling sick. It's all image, nothing that lasts."

Then a loud pickup truck rumbled by, the open back filled with yet more blonds, this time of the male persuasion. They were whooping at each other and raising their beer cans at side-walkers as if being in traffic was something to celebrate.

"Aren't they smart?" said the singer. "We call them organ donors."

Most people were heading toward the central courtyard for fireworks. Some of the guys were shirtless, painted red and white, wearing university flags as capes. Some of the gals were in tight sparkly shorts or pleated skirts. The procession was loud and colourful, a practice celebration in case genuine celebration was required some day. Mindless, I couldn't help thinking, but also oddly purposeful. The stuck smiles and pumping fists passed us by, a moving picture of politicians and bank execs-to-be in their masks of youth learning to play the fool on the way to becoming king.

The scene was foreign to my experience. The university I had attended in Toronto was like a massive high school. There was neither a football stadium nor a team. The school didn't even have its own hockey arena. The pride that did exist was muted by the fact that the school was deep in the heart of a cosmopolitan city where voices were many and few of them were loud. I could, though, relate to the male bonding drunkenness. And I did know about the awkward timing of deciding how you might care to be different while being asked to follow along.

The singer and I took a position near the clock tower in time for the first loud cracks and showers of silver light. Apparently if ISU beat Texas they would have a shot at their first-ever bowl game. Much was on the line, then: the justification of funding, maintenance of alumni support, a touch of national attention. After the show, the marching band contributed brass and bravado, sending the mob away on a high. A couple standing near us was limb-locked and engaged in a long kiss. A few footballers walked past, beer cans poorly concealed by their sides.

My companion sighed. "People succumb so easily to temptation," she said sarcastically.

"Do you think sex and drugs are the apple?" I asked.

She smiled. Then, digging a hand out of her sweater's deep pocket, she swatted me on the shoulder. "You got it," she said. "Satan convinced Eve to eat the apple."

After that, I wondered, did Eve convince Adam to taste her pie? A dastardly thought I didn't voice because I didn't feel like getting hit again. "That's not very Christ-like," she might have said. He did love both women and wine, though, and he might have appreciated a little joke about Eve's pie.

The singer walked me to the bus stop. These were our final minutes. We hadn't discussed Jesus Christ the person versus Jesus Christ the set of ideas, or debated faith acquired alone and over time versus faith handed down from one generation to the next like antique furniture. I could have at least echoed the Chi Alpha flyer—*free your mind*—but I didn't. I would let her direct the ending.

She was talking about what she wanted to be when she grew up; something that involved helping or healing, perhaps a psychiatrist or massage therapist.

"Your future is like a gift under the tree," she said. "Although God's not like Santa Claus. Some people think He is, but I don't. You can't compare anything to Him. He is *the* example, and everything follows His pattern, or hopes to. *Everything* is some small or large reflection of Him."

Religion was the only good-times proposition for her: prayer and worship the party, God the drug. I fished for some appropriate final words. "Are you happy with your place in the world?"

"I'm happy to be here," she said. "Who wouldn't be? I feel a lot of anticipation about what's to come. I think everyone is just a work-in-progress."

We waited in silence until the bus arrived to take me in the direction of the motel where I had a room. As with the widow, I would never see the singer again. Our affiliation had ended.

On the way out of central Ames the next day, I looked back to see the roadside sign again, to confirm that I hadn't imagined it. It was still there, this time waiting for me in full: JESUS IS YOUR FRIEND. The new message was more appropriate to the environs. While few Iowans (I assume) would claim to be Jesus, many, including the singer, would say they were good buddies. Still, I felt a little disappointed, a little disillusioned. We see only what we're predisposed to see, whether good, bad or saintly. Both versions were agreeable, but should my faith lie with the first reading or the second? Poster or prophecy, I had to wonder. If I wasn't Jesus reincarnate, at least I knew he was on the team, a solid linebacker on my holy offense.

I had shrugged the matter off by the time the bus was roaring up to freeway speed. Des Moines or, better yet, Kansas City, here I come. One god or another was along for the ride. And he—or she, or it— was always in a different disguise.

18

A hush descended on the bus station in Kansas City when two DEA agents walked through the front doors. One of the anti-drug officers had a tight leash-grip on a sleek and muscular German shepherd. The threesome walked between the two sections of seating, seemingly headed for the washrooms. The hush didn't last long: the men were noticed by most of us who were waiting, registered as an unsurprising detail, and then ignored.

The bus to St. Louis, via Columbia, was scheduled to leave in five minutes. I had decided to go to Columbia. My mother had been born there, when my grandfather, Walter, was working at the University of Missouri. They had lived on a street called Sunset Lane. Admittedly, that data was faint motivation. Mom didn't care whether I stopped there or not. She had no memories of the place; the family had left town when she was a toddler; they headed for upper-state New York, and eventually Ontario. However, I was now a mere 110 miles away. Why not swing by? Columbia, simply, could be a destination like any other.

A rotund black bus driver entered the station. "St. Louis!" he barked.

I stood, and shouldered my backpack. The DEA agents exited the men's washroom. One of them—the officer not in charge of the dog—was wearing dark sunglasses, and I thought I heard him sniff as he marched past me. From my place in line, I watched the authorities leave the way they came in.

It was a Sunday afternoon during the NFL season, and we were soon passing Arrowhead Stadium, where the Chiefs and the St. Louis Rams were about to heave and grunt in formation. The parking lot, bigger than five football fields, was full, and the corporate blimps were congregating (both in the sky and in reserved seating). Some of the excitement and anticipation had leaked onto the bus.

"Who they playing?"

"The Rams."

"Oh. They'll win."

"You nuts?"

"I ain't bettin', but you gotta cheer for the home team."

"When you done cheerin', face reality: the Chiefs are lousy."

"It don't matter. Our day's gonna come."

"Bah."

I was next to a young guy who had left Tri-Cities, Washington, forty-eight hours before. His hair was a mangy collection of dense curls, and he wore glasses: a studious misfit. He would drift off for ten minutes at a time.

"Wah?" he said, coming out of the slumber. He looked toward the stadium. "Football." He twitched his brow spastically a few times, said he was having trouble blinking, that his eyelids weren't cooperating. "The lack of sleep is starting to mess with my mind."

He lifted himself up to scan the length of the bus. "I have to say I prefer the train to this. You can at least move around while you're moving."

He was on his way to Joplin, Missouri, to fill in for a couple of weeks for a friend at a tattoo and body piercing shop. He had four rings in his lower lip, one in the upper, a stainless steel nail through his tongue, and three hoops hanging from each ear lobe. And, unsurprisingly, he was an itinerant, a free spirit. He was going to try and be home again for Thanksgiving, after maybe dropping by Louisiana on the way. Longer term, his plan was to pass the winter on various Mexican beaches.

"People at home don't understand," he said. "They're like, 'Ah, leaving again, eh, you lazy fucker. Where are you quitting to this time?' And it's not like that. You work hard to put a purse together, and then you go some place and spend it slowly. They think when you're out in the world it's all freedom and joy, skipping across the sand, drunk on coconut milk or whatever, when travel is actually a lot of work." He silenced himself with a yawn. "Christ, get me off this bus. But it's always a trip, right?"

I nodded. A trip, a hodgepodge of visuals and sound bites, a long and thick tale of idiosyncratic seconds.

At the next rest stop, the driver walked back to the bus carrying a plastic box. He was hugging the package next to his side with one arm, like a football. During the final minutes before reboarding, I tried to get a better look at the box. The body piercer was next to me, attempting to sleep while standing up. The package was important-looking, white and marked with large red crosses, *Handle With Care* written in black across the side. Then the driver switched the weight to his other hand, and I saw more. HUMAN EYE. I nudged my tattooist friend.

"Jesus," he said. "Glad I'm not the guy going blind waiting on that delivery."

His smile was killed by a yawn.

We had stopped for two minutes on the fringes of a gas station halfway between Kansas City and Columbia. As we hit the interstate on-ramp, a woman sitting near me was anxious for the driver's attention.

"Excuse me, sir," she called toward the front of the bus. "Sir? Hello!"

The driver looked up into the rear-view mirror. "What?"

"I think we're missing someone," said the woman. "An old lady got off back there."

"Yeah?"

"She didn't get back on."

"What the hell," said the driver. He signalled us into traffic.

"She didn't get back on," the woman said again more quietly, probably curious—as I was—about whether we'd be turning around. The driver was silent, his anger battling his guilt, perhaps, although not for long. I noticed a roadside sign that indicated the next exit wasn't for twenty miles, so maybe the quandary solved itself.

The driver's voice crackled over the P.A. "Let this be a lesson to the rest of you," he said. "I said that wasn't a rest stop. I always make that clear. Do I have to lock everyone in here? The next bus will have to get her. That mistake will cost her a five-hour layover."

At the two-bench depot in Ames, I had received an explanation for why the occasional driver was hard-boiled. I was standing with a ticket agent and we were watching through the window as passengers bustled around. Some people were getting off to stay, a few were just off to smoke or stretch, a third group was waiting to board. The driver was short, bow-legged and muscular, an old bulldog.

"A lot of these drivers are ex-cops or ex-military," the agent said. "They're getting older, but they still want to be working, to be doing something."

The driver started throwing baggage into the bus's hold. He could just as easily have been loading artillery onto a jeep or tossing rucksacks into a helicopter.

The agent stuck his hands in his pockets. Shook his head. "See this guy?" he said. "He wouldn't take any shit from anyone. They're into that whole authority thing; they've been in charge of one thing or another their entire lives."

The new passengers were lined up near the open door, their tickets pinched in hand like draft cards. Family members stood at close range, waiting for the last kiss and for a wave goodbye.

We hurtled eastbound through central Missouri, now with one less passenger. The old lady's carry-on bags, one cotton and one plastic, were occupying her seat, sadly suggesting that if you're not on the highway, you're learning the hard way. I thought about the old lady, imagined her alarm and agitation. I was glad not to be her, frankly, relieved that *my* day hadn't just descended into dreary chaos.

With selfish pleasure I relished my own good fortune. The plains, I noticed, were no longer dominant. The land was lush with trees and rippled as if a primordial stew once bubbled below the earth and the ground had remained in that mould, in the wavy contours of wind-blown sand. I sat back and absorbed the latest geography. Soon I'd be in Columbia, moving on.

I dawdled in downtown Columbia, hoping for an episode. After dark, a man wearing sunglasses and a black leather jacket approached me on the sidewalk. He appeared shrunken; I could see rib-lines through his stretchy tank top. He had a beard and shoulder-length hair, and carried a gnarled wooden staff. Charlie Deuce, as he called himself, was the thirsty urban nomad, and these streets were his desert.

"There are good people all over," he said. "Interesting people. You just gotta be looking for them. I'm on my way to see the boys right now if you wanna join me."

We headed down an active avenue. Friday night was coming to life with distraction-seekers. Vehicles were being driven slowly so the occupants could inspect each other, the point not to get home in a blind rush but to idle and eyeball. A gaggle of painted and powdered girls was lined up outside a dance club, each one an individual balancing act of high heels and hot pants.

"How you ladies doing tonight?" said Deuce. He fancied himself a real charmer. He also had no concern for what the world might be thinking.

One of the girls said "okay" quietly. They exchanged a mental note with smiling glances—*ugh, did you see his teeth?*—then turned to see themselves in the tinted window, anxious to be encased in the thump-thump darkness. Their temporary location turned out to be our destination: a bench outside the bar. Two men were sitting there; one was awake and alert, the other passed out crookedly.

"Sleeping Beauty is with us again," said Deuce as the folded man started to sit up. "That's Stretch. And this here is Lone Wolf. I picked up a straggler, boys."

I shook hands with Lone Wolf. Another beard, but only jeans and T-shirt for a uniform. The shirt pictured a mother cradling a child in front of a sunset. Lone Wolf kept a little change in his pocket by crafting wire jewelry. He had a pair of pliers in hand; a bagful of copper was on the ground next to him.

"He can do anything you want," said Deuce. "Made to order." He held out the copper cross he was wearing around his neck that Lone Wolf had twisted into shape.

Lone Wolf nodded. "Name it and I'll try it."

"How about an owl?" I said.

He let the detail sink in. "Okay. I'll give it a try."

Stretch grumbled to life and responded to the loud reverberations with anger. "This is all wrong," he said. "Give me the old stuff. Give me Buddy Holly. Give me Elvis."

Lone Wolf got up from the bench and stepped up to the imaginary mike, in this case his pliers, leaning toward Deuce for effect. "Wise men saa-y, only fools rush in. But I… can't… help… falling in love with you."

Stretch removed his *Goodbye Tension Hello Pension* ball cap, scratched his head and yawned. He had shared his last opinion of the night. Deuce decided to take charge of the congregation. "How about we mosey around the corner and leave the rest of these folks to their fantasy?"

"You have a bottle?" asked Lone Wolf.

Deuce nodded and turned to me. "Shall we retire to my office?"

I fell in slow step behind the threesome, and noticed that Stretch was not merely bowlegged; his right leg was actually shaped like a bow: the knee didn't bend at all, and he carried it like a scythe, swinging the stiff limb forward with each step. He had been hit by a train.

"He just wanted a ride, but it rolled over him," said Deuce, turning to flash a broken-tooth smile. "He's the only guy I know who can put his leg over his head."

Stretch just grunted. We walked to a public parking area behind the main street buildings. The far side of the lot had a three-foot wall that made for suitable sitting. We took places below a city ordinance sign. IF YOU PARK HERE YOU WILL BE TOWED. From one end I leaned forward and looked along the line of us. I noticed that Deuce was wearing green and black combat boots.

"Were you in the service?"

"Eyes like an owl, right!" he said. "I was a chopper pilot in Vietnam. I slipped into these for the first time over thirty years ago."

Out came the little brown paper bag. One mouth at a time went to the drink like buckets to the community well. I didn't know what it was until the liquid hit my tongue: vodka. It was sharp and went down ugly, warming on a warm night.

"Are the memories faded?"

Deuce's half-smile told me I was naive, but he didn't seem to mind the question. "If you told me it was just a long dream I had one time, I might believe you; if you told me it was a nightmare I shared with friends, I'd know you was telling the truth."

Lone Wolf looked over at me to see if he had my attention. "One time we came into one of them hamlets and a few snipers popped up behind us," he said. "I was sitting on the tank and took a bullet right in the ass. It ricocheted." He continued to twist the wire as he talked. "Then we... Well, once we got straightened out, we decided to level the place," he said. "All we found after was three women and a bunch of kids. That wasn't good for me, for my mind."

He looked up when Stretch placed the brown bag in his field of vision. After swigging decently Lone Wolf grimaced: a brief, deranged grin. "My uncle served in Korea, my father served in World War II, my grandfather served in World War One. We're all friendly folks, but we all fought for this country. I think we need to get a good march going. This country's got no concern for its countrymen."

He let loose with a cough his mother would have worried about. I wouldn't probe further. I wasn't sure what else was to be gained from the recollections. (What, for that matter, had been the night's profit thus far? I was feeling blessed, lucky that I had no scars to show, or to talk about, lucky I had two working legs, lucky I was drinking not to forget, but rather to warp reality and make it differently memorable.) Deuce closed the topic.

"Wars, wars, wars," he said. "You know what I wonder? Why do people have to be so cruel to people? We were put here to need each other, to protect each other. It's not about saving the world. It's about being decent, helping a brother who needs help. Listen to this," he said, tapping my hand. "It's better to be Christ-like than to just like Christ."

"I like that," I said. His words were a bent echo of the message I read in Ames: better, in Deuce's mind, to pretend Jesus is you than to pretend He's your friend.

Deuce shrugged. "I preach at Presbyterian, Methodist, First Christian. Any of 'em. It don't matter. The message don't change." He paused and cracked a smile. "But my sunglasses do. I wear darker ones when I'm giving a sermon."

Lone Wolf stood up and walked over to me. The project was finished.

"I like using my hands to build something that didn't exist before," he said. He passed me the shaped wire. "Let me tell you one thing," he said. "I say it to all my customers: machines don't need to make money, machines don't have families. You always know when something's handmade. Good or bad, it's an act of creation."

I insisted that his work was indeed good and offered to provide the next half-pint of vodka, as payment.

"Only pay what you can," he said. "What you think is necessary." And without a moment's hesitation he gave me directions to a nearby store. My conscience wasn't disturbed as I perused the shelves of cheap and hard liquor at the corner market. College boys buzzed around me, hunting their own breed of numbness. I could have paid for the owl in cash, but this way I saved Lone Wolf the short walk. A bottle was central to the scene, along with the unsteady hands and floating ruby eyes. They had little, but they had little together, which should beat having a lot alone. I envied their alliance, as rummy and fragile as it was. (And I myself was willing to continue drinking. Happy to.) I took my selection to the counter.

A serious discussion was underway when I returned. Deuce was pointing down at a small Bible, which was sitting face up on the ground near his booted feet. "Show me where it says I can't do what I want to do."

"You can't strip on the governor's car," said Lone Wolf.

"It don't say that."

And Stretch just grunted.

I asked them to back up a little and fill me in. Deuce was the clown of this small class (complete with bulbous red nose). On Halloween a couple of years before he had jumped onto the governor's car and stripped down to a pair of ladies' blue satin panties. He was promising to repeat the feat this year, and that night was wearing the same panties. He flashed them to us as a story prop.

The new bottle was passed from Lone Wolf's hands and arrived in Deuce's. "The Lord never said we shouldn't drink, He never said we shouldn't smoke. Abuse anything and it will kill you. The Lord don't need to tell us that. But He never said we shouldn't be who we are."

Lone Wolf took the bottle, which had become the conversational baton. "They tell me to move along and I move along. That's what happened to the Son of God. Jesus was never accepted anywhere He went."

"Wolf here has always been moving from spot to spot," said Deuce. "He moves to survive."

"Yep," said Lone Wolf. "I been to Peoria, Illa-noise, Decatur, Illa-noise, Chicago, Illa-noise, Macon, Missoura, Jefferson City, Missoura, and now Columbia, Missoura. I'm gonna see most of the world before it can finish me."

We absorbed his words. Sobering thoughts were the specialty of wasted people. From time to time, the conversation stopped altogether, and we sat in silence, four men in a row on a concrete bench. What were they thinking? Were they considering blunders, victories, historical opportunities, the various ways they had arrived at that place on that night? The ways they had failed to arrive elsewhere? Were they curious what would happen next?

On the way back to the peace and cable TV of my motel cell, I wondered what it would be like to have a war behind you, to know precisely how shrapnel diced flesh, or how bullets got lost in the wash of pumping blood. Two lines came back to me. Both Lone Wolf and Charlie Deuce had smiled: the rehearsed act of a comedic duo.

"We gave our lives," said Lone Wolf.

"Yeah," said Deuce. "But we ain't dead yet."

And Stretch grunted.

20

On a day that might have been torn from a retiree magazine (artful shade, a breeze crafting the leaves), I walked outward from Columbia's core. I passed first through the minimum wage part of town, where letting paint peel and driveways crumble didn't offend the neighbours. A message was scrawled in black marker on somebody's white front door: *You don't live here.* I assumed the warning was directed at repeat intruders who decided they felt at home.

I marched ahead into the landscape of the middle class, where the envy that continued to grow was kept tidy and pruned. One large house set far back on a large front lawn featured two thick and proud whitewashed columns. A stone lion stood at the base of each one, a ripe pumpkin under the nose of each chiselled animal, identical pots of gardenias on every step up to the door. The stars and stripes fluttered gently from a pole on each pillar. In sum, a disturbing symmetry of comfort symbols, a cultivated calm. Home as people would like to remember it.

Ostensibly, I was looking for Sunset Lane. "I always thought the name was perfect," Mom had said when I suggested I might try to locate the house where her family lived when she was born. The problem was I had neither a house number nor a reasonable description of what the house might look like. The family had left town fifty-five years before.

I marched on. Porch swings swayed with tired ghosts. Dying leaves were blown off their branches to the sidewalk where passing feet crunched them to pieces and then powder. Acorns pattered on the ground intermittently like the end of rain. I walked and walked. I had a city map, and I thought I was going in the right direction, but I stepped into a drugstore to confirm my bearings.

"Sunset Lane?" said the clerk, a middle-aged woman. "Sure, you're within a mile of it from here." She looked down at my map for a moment. "No more than two."

My half-hearted search for Sunset Lane was over. I began winding my way back to the city. Sunset Lane simply wasn't my past. Midtown Columbia was, however, my present. In the distance, I could hear the shrill barks of an angry dog. Then, perhaps in response, the extended howls of a lonely dog. I came up to a house with several cars parked out front, and heard singing. *Happy Birthday to Leslie, Happy Birthday to you.* The song was followed by a cheer and clapping. I glanced over the cedar fence as I walked past. The backyard was studded with people and plastic furniture. I couldn't see Leslie, though, or the candled cake held to her nose.

A few blocks later, I witnessed the end of a father's tirade. He was upset with his son's mismanagement of the garden hose. He looked down at the woman next to him who was on her knees in a flowerbed. "Did you see this?" he said. "Did you? He tangled it up every goddamn which way. Christ. How much does he get for allowance, anyway? Huh?" The man paused for a moment, held out the hose from his body like it was a sinister eel. "Hey," he said. "You're not listening." The woman—his wife, I assumed—never looked up from her work with the trowel. However, she must have said something. "Twenty?" said the man. "Twenty bucks. Christ. And the little bastard thinks he's earning it—"

The man noticed that I was listening; I didn't look away in time. His eyes held mine, and seemed to ask if I dare think his anger wasn't justified.

I hurried to leave the scene behind.

Downtown again, I claimed a patch of grass on the campus quad at the University of Missouri. I was the only person loitering in such a manner, an emptiness that seemed out of the ordinary for such a warm and clear afternoon. Oh, well: more open space for the drifter. I lay spread-eagled on the turf, and tried to shake the memory of that father's short fuse. I wondered: Had their love been brilliant once upon a time? Was the man hard by nature? Was the woman bored with him or them or the city? And was their son a victim, or would he be a challenge for even the most wily and determined parents?

People fired the imagination.

Might my girlfriend and I have walked a similar garden path toward happily ever after? Would the lawn-care lifestyle have made *me* a difficult man?

"I wouldn't want to live like you," said my mother before I flew out of Ontario. We were talking about my tendency to stray, and the way I resisted planning ahead. "But I'm confident that you'll figure it out."

I didn't ask her what "it" was. My mother's mother, God bless her well-intentioned soul, was less understanding about what she saw as my perpetual dilly-dallying. "I wish you would find something that you'd like to do in a place you'd like to be."

My grandmother used some version of that line every time I talked to her. *Find something to do.* I didn't ask whether a three-month bus ride qualified as a valid activity. My choices confused her; she couldn't compartmentalize me.

The older people in my life, my elders, implored me to spend my time wisely (implying that I was doing no such thing); they also said, at a frequency correlated to age, that they didn't know where their lives had gone.

Although my grandmother knew the value of travel—visiting a certain place is often near the top of the list of things people wish they had done—she was certain that I was putting off the acquisition of a real life. About this she was partly correct. I *assumed* I would one day embark on the journey of infinite payments known as a mortgage. I *supposed* I might grow tired of my elective poverty (and the guilt I carried from relying on certain family members) and experiment with a career (pressed pants, ham sandwiches at noon, economic self-sufficiency).

All three of my siblings had their own homes; their prospective paths were laid out clearly. I was the youngest child, the only arrow still fluttering through airspace strewn with options. To my brothers and sister, I was an amusing curiosity. They applauded my schemes: no one was shocked when I announced my desire to cross, by bus, two of the largest countries in the world. My psychology professor brother once told me about a birth order theory that became the seed of stereotype. The youngest child was spoiled, rebellious, unconventional, all of which were somewhat true in my case. The conscientious high achievers came before me, those who played by more and stricter rules.

From a vacant field I stared skyward, past the margins of grey buildings and gruff cars, past treetops and bird sound, pretending I could do more than fly, pretending I was a space age busboy who made himself indispensable to the heavens by learning how to exhale clouds that could bear the weight of a stout god, pretending—

"Excuse me, sir."

I sat up, shielding my eyes from the afternoon sun. I was looking at the chest of a member of the school's security squad.

"Sorry," he said. "We're trying to let the grass grow. I'm gonna have to ask you to move."

So I did.

21

Heading west from Columbia, I noticed an exit sign for a town called Prairie Home. Maybe I was ten miles from a glorious end: wife singing in the backyard bathtub, barefoot son chasing daughter in torn dress, laundered sheets swaying on the line, porch and rocker and sweaty beverage, hours creaking forward, hours creaking back. Names could be exceptional advertising.

I wouldn't experience Prairie Home, though, and not only because the exit was already two minutes behind us. I had a specific agenda. I was on my way back to Kansas City, where I was going to see a woman who shared her home with twenty crocodiles. I had received the tip from a girl waiting at the depot in Columbia who used to help out with the exotic pets.

"If you're within 500 miles of Kansas City, you owe it to yourself to meet her," she said.

I could have gone eastbound, continued chatting with the girl on the way to St. Louis. She likely had advice for that city as well. But I had little doubt the crocodile lady would be worth retracing a couple of hours on the I-70. I was happy to take a tip from a stranger.

I briefly lost my bearings in suburban Kansas City.

From downtown, I rode half an hour on a metro bus (graffiti-signed vinyl seats, poor people hugging bags of groceries, jarring, squealing stops every block). I got off and started walking east on the street I thought would take me to the avenue I was looking for. I walked up hills and down hills. I crossed one-way streets and four-lane thoroughfares. Eventually I would have considered trading my compass for a detailed map of the neighbourhood that bound me.

I had an appointment to keep, so I sought direction from two young boys approaching on their bicycles. The area was quiet, oddly car-free in the afternoon, and I was walking along near the middle of the road.

"Can you guys tell me where Euclid Avenue is?" I said.

One turned and started back. "We're not supposed to talk to strangers," he said.

The second boy was circling behind the first. I stopped walking, and they began to ride around me in a wide circle. The kid who spoke was in the lead, the second boy giggling as he pedalled to keep up.

"So you know where it is, but you can't tell me?" I said.

"*Don't talk to strangers.*" He said it in a high voice I assumed was a mimicry of his mother's. After another circle they raced down the street, talking and laughing. They were comfortable enough in their own neighbourhood that strangers were less a threat than a joke, a temporary alien amusement.

We were all told to be wary of strangers. Would I stop to help a stranger like myself? I hoped so. I walked on.

The subdivision seemed tired, beaten-down. Here a camper trailer resting on piled bricks. There a corroded sedan with soft tires, sinking slowly into the dirt lawn. Everywhere plastic and scrap building materials in small mounds like garbage that won't be used, won't be removed. Many homes had barred windows, and some residents had barbed wire across the top of their perimeter fence. I was reminded of gated communities, and condominiums patrolled by rent-a-cops, where residents fork out for a sense of safety, for the mere feeling that worldly evil couldn't possibly find them where they live. Fear could be costly.

By the laws of chance and inevitability, I soon arrived at Euclid. A long white passenger van was parked on the corner with hazard lights flashing and stylized lettering across its side. *Cutting Edge Ministries: Presenting a living Jesus to a dying world.*

In the three seconds it took me to wonder where the driver was, two of the van's occupants turned toward me from the end of the nearest driveway. They were boys, not yet old enough to shave, and they were tidy, from the shiny shoes, navy slacks and blazers, to the bright teeth and short, combed hair. They looked like a pair of Antichrists.

"How are you today, friend?" said one.

"Fine," I said. "How are you guys?"

"Good," said the other. "Can we ask you a couple of questions?"

"Actually, I'm already late for a meeting."

"Are you sure?"

"Yeah," I said, stepping between them. "Sorry."

Not a lie, more like a mechanical brush-off. On my childhood crescent, parents hustled their kids inside and drew the curtains when a pair of dark-suited men were spotted going from door to door with pamphlets drawn like weapons. I was taught to run from robotic missionary types. From a safe distance, I turned around for another look. Now who was scared? Perhaps I wasn't scared, but I was definitely unsettled, troubled that people had license to make house calls for the purpose of injecting fables into the veins of vulnerable souls.

And I was made uneasy by a vision: those navy suits dragging me into their white van, escorting me blindfolded to a rural basement (I would hear dripping; I would smell mould) where, using several cold and spiky instruments, they would lobotomize those inches of my brain that made me a self-satisfied heathen.

With silent, matching strides, they turned up the next driveway. I supposed I had fled from abnormal and valuable quotes. But I had already gathered unto me the singer from Ames. How many of God's children were too many? I smiled. Crossed my fingers. Crossed the street.

On Euclid Avenue, I found the house I was looking for before I saw its number. The unpruned bushes were swollen to the full width of the sidewalk, tickling the curb. I had to walk on the street to find the gap in the hedge where the gate was. The entire property was a micro-jungle, the house itself mostly concealed by a thick wrapping of vines and overgrown trees.

I could hear birds inside, a raucous chorus. I opened the screen and pounded on the inside door. She was expecting me, but probably couldn't hear the knock, so I decided to compete with the wildlife and started shouting. The birds quieted briefly as though curious who the weird human was. Eventually the crocodile lady arrived at the door.

"Come on in," she said. "I'll put you to work."

I left my pack by the door. I had to turn my body and shuffle sideways in order to pass through the front room. Large steel tubs occupied most of the floor space, and from the tubs to the ceiling was an elaborate transit system of wire pathways. I heard muffled splashing as I passed between the board-covered tubs.

The birds behind the wires were macaws, with aqua blue plumage and bright yellow bellies. Their chattering was high-pitched and crotchety. Garbage cans turned on their sides were affixed to the ceiling as nests, and, via the wide tubes of caging material, the birds passed more freely than a person could from one room to another.

I caught up to the crocodile lady in the kitchen. She was short, thick, and bowlegged, a standing bull. Her silver hair, corralled with an elastic band and reaching down to the small of her back, looked like the tangled tail of an old horse. One of her hands was inside a cage, scratching the head of a crow. The bird's beak was crossed just as my fingers had been minutes ago; one of its claws was twisted up like excess wire.

"You might as well meet the cast," said my host. "This is Tiffy. Say hello, Tiffy."

And it did. The maimed crow said, "Hello."

"God only knows what happened to her," said the crocodile lady. "The doctor said nothing damaged like that should survive. That was fifteen years ago. The doctor has since died of cancer."

A parrot leaned into the open window next to the sink. "Pear-rot! Pear-rot!"

"Oh, Jesus. John Silver, you have to be a part of everything, don't you?"

"Hello," said Tiffy again, anxious to make my acquaintance.

"Uh, hello," I said, to the house in general. I felt like a rare human guest on an unscripted television show where the animals were the stars. I turned around and looked into the glass eyes of a giant stuffed marlin hanging on the wall. "Some sonavabitch got a thrill killing that fish," said the crocodile lady. "It needs dusting." Inside the front door was one of those bison heads only appropriate on the walls of rural taverns. I also noticed a stuffed red parrot perched on a branch outside the macaw cages.

We walked around the tight maze of her home, and she introduced me to her reptilian children. One was lounging on the boards above its tub in the spare bedroom. It was like a long, intricately carved stone. The creature didn't move or blink, made not the slightest suggestion that it was alive. We went from room to room; many of the other crocodiles were out of sight, circling quietly in the darkness of the covered tubs. Twiggy and Cutie and Grendel... A total of twenty-four caimans lived in the house, a breed whose natural habitat was South American rainforest. I asked about the slender-stalked plants that were a tropical spray of green in every room.

"It's papyrus and I don't think I could kill it if I tried," she said. "It divided into two, then divided into four. I think I've got sixteen now."

The crocodile lady's son had brought home one of the first reptiles in a sandwich bag. That croc lived twenty years and had seven kids. Once she answered the door and a young man was standing there with a crocodile in his arms. "The stupid bugger was building machine guns," she said. "He says to me, 'I have to go to Leavenworth for eighteen months. Here's Killer.' And he never came back." Most of the crocodiles were born and raised in her house, the only place, she said, where the species had ever reproduced in captivity. While caimans reached only four or five feet at maturity, a true monster lived in the basement, next to the washing machine. He was the lone alligator tenant, an eleven-footer named Hojo.

"How are we feeling today, Hojo?" said the crocodile lady when we went downstairs for a visit. Hojo had no comment. He just stared at me, maybe curious what the pale and bony male would taste like.

We went back up to the kitchen and into the backyard. Catalpa trees, densely festooned with shoots like green pencils, formed the dense perimeter. Hojo and the crocs entered and exited the house via a series of ramps and windows that were modified into swinging doors. Birdhouses decorated every tree trunk and twenty or more pigeons were perched along the power lines running from the house.

"Everyone's a little anxious today," said the crocodile lady. "We've had a few deaths in the family."

Sometime during the previous night a predator had nabbed seven pigeons, including Baldy and his wife Miss Pretty, both of whom had been with her for twenty years. Whether cat or raccoon, "the goddamn thing has to be caught," she grumbled. I helped her haul out the Havahart trap from beside the house and set it with a can of cat food. She expected the enemy would return that night.

"When the animal's a killer you're not doing anybody any favours," she said. "But I'm not gonna kill it, so I gotta find a home for it."

She showed me where some of the birdcages needed repair and reinforcement, handed me a staple gun, and went off to feed her chickens. She was followed to the roost by a pesky African gander. He waddled behind her, pleading with a nasal croak.

"Oh, Squeaky, don't act so sad. You're not alone. We're all one-of-a-kind around here."

"Pear-rot! Pear-rot!"

She turned and yelled toward the house. "Relax, John Silver! Will you relax? I'm coming. Can't entertain yourself for thirty seconds."

Every living thing was asserting its presence. Every individual had to be accounted for, fed, talked to, even the rat that scurried past my feet. I assumed that it was an uninvited guest, until she said he belonged like the rest.

"He's blind, but he takes care of himself just fine. Rats will be here long after we've poisoned ourselves."

The crocodile lady didn't have a television, VCR, or microwave—not a single apparatus that beeped. She seemed to put little trust in the constructs of modern civilization. Her world was decorated with only breathing (or formerly breathing) ornaments. She was someone Noah could have called when his feet started to get wet, unless he was short on cats and dogs, of which she had none. The cat, in fact, was the pet that peeved her the most.

"Nineteen million songbirds a year are killed by cats in Wisconsin," she said. "There was a boy in Cape Cod who said about the songbirds, 'Mommy, do they eat flowers? They sing so sweet.' Thoreau wrote that, you know."

"Pear-rot! Pear-rot!"

"Oh, Jesus," she said. "It never ends. Every daylight hour of every day."

"Do you think you have more than you can handle?" I asked.

She shrugged. "I collect things. That's my problem. Things that need me."

That was as close as I would get to an explanation of why: why the crocs, why the birds, why the private zoo in residential Kansas City. Maybe there was a breed of people who understood the human animal least. A species that identified more closely with worms turning through soil, or turtles basking on flat rock, or spiders casting lines of web, than they did with cosmetic chatterers waiting impatiently for a double shot of espresso and one more biscotti. The crocodile lady didn't question the way she was living any more than anyone else did. I might have pursued illumination. *Let the beavers build dams, for chrissake!* she might have said. *It's what they do.*

Her populated home was quiet at dusk. I could hear the pigeons outside, their soft warble of sleep.

"I hope the birds will be okay tonight," she said. As she wiped her forehead with tissue I realized she had rarely stopped talking (to me or her family) during my visit, and never sat down. Her eyelids were dark and heavy, her back bent and shoulders slumped. "John Silver, are you in bed?"

The parrot answered by entering via the kitchen window. With two quick flaps he winged from the counter to her shoulder. The crocodile lady looked like a lost pirate who preferred to remain adrift, a rogue, beyond the touch of time or place. She leaned against the plant-filled sink with one hand.

"It's a goddamn monkey asylum in here," she said.

The parrot leaned forward and turned to look her in the eye. "Who's a pretty bird!" it said. "Who's a pretty bird!"

And behind us Tiffy the crow said, "Hello."

Even humans, being alive and vulnerable as anything else that grew up on earth, were granted some of the crocodile lady's care. She pushed a few small bills into my hand for helping to fix the cages. She fed me leftovers. She wanted to know where I was staying while in Kansas City. When I said I had neither a bed nor an itinerary, she nodded, and got on the phone to her current support staff. A woman named Stacy, who, thanks to the crocodile lady, had gained experience tending to needy creatures, agreed to take me in. She said she'd be right over.

Then I was in the warm cab of a pickup truck, racing toward a midtown tenement, warbling a chorus with Mick Jagger, and agreeing with my escort Stacy that it was a nice night, yes indeed, and maybe a couple six-packs of Sol were in order. (She said she had a stoop that invited lounging.)

Stacy was about my age. Though Kansas City was home, she had seen plenty of what she called "preferable America." In her mind, Missouri was no match for Colorado, Nevada, or New Mexico. She loved to drive and drive, coast with The Boss and Willie Nelson, sail gaily over the Rio Grande, part the calm red desert, stop when the cold of dark crashed in, nestle with a man or blankets in the back of her truck under a star-kicking sky.

"I love leaving," she said.

The statement cemented our temporary friendship. Like the tattoo artist from Washington, Stacy was another kindred soul. We sat looking over her squat backyard, where she and her roommate parked their vehicles, and where more catalpa trees drooped beneath the pallid orange of big city night. We talked about where else we could be. Alaska, India, Morocco. The inventory ended with Mexico, that cheap and sun-scorched hideaway of lore. I summarized my modest travels, my short history of going. She understood, without it being articulated, how movement was a matter of survival to me, how I considered myself separated only by the distance of time from the hunter/gatherers found frozen now and then in out-of-the-way mountain passes. The moment she laid eyes on me—"that hat of yours has been around, hasn't it?"—Stacy suspected I was afraid to fix myself anywhere.

For herself, for now, Stacy was pleased enough to stay put. She had two agreeable jobs in the city. In addition to working for the crocodile lady, she repaired Persian rugs. Perhaps the chief cause of her current inertia was the fact she adored someone.

"He's sweet, he listens, he makes me peaceful," she said. "He's someone I would follow."

As tentative youth softened by beer, we talked openly between extended silences. We talked about figuring out what was essential. We couldn't help but consider archetypal love.

I slept two nights on Stacy's living room floor. I wandered the streets while she was knitting careful knots at the rug shop. On the morning of the third day, while Stacy was in the shower and I was gathering my things to go, a message was left on her answering machine.

"Stacy! The ugliest goddamn sonavabitch of a raccoon is in the dog trap. He's horrible but we got him. When can you come over?"

After admitting she thought her boss was a little strange, Stacy made plans to drop by the crocodile lady's house and help allay this most recent crisis. First, though, she would deliver me to the bus station so that I could, in her words, "continue making headway." As though my trip were a task, a mission. I nodded. We left.

I looked over my shoulder through the filthy window of the cab. A light rain was falling on weekday Kansas City, and on my pack in the back of the truck. I wondered how long I would sit at the station. Where to next? At such moments my journey carried the heaviness of assignment. All I hoped to do was to populate my environment with those who were lively, loud, damaged—somehow set apart. But I could hardly force such uncommonness into every new foreground.

Stacy and I were quiet in the truck. I wanted to tell her how fortunate I was to have met her, and how I'd be pleased to run into her one day at a random crossroads in the desert. We were relaxed together, I thought. I could be myself with her. Although the fact I felt at ease was worth celebrating, I managed to resist any possibly embarrassing exclamations. The grey day had made us both shy. Rain-listeners. Stacy must have thought I was dwelling on the decision I still had to make. "What about Branson?" she said.

"Branson?"

"Yeah. The Nashville of the Ozarks, I think they call it. Branson's fucked up."

I took a moment to absorb her sales pitch. "Why not?" I said.

When we got to the station, Stacy kept the engine running for a short goodbye.

22

Salvation battled sin on the billboards of a highway cutting through Mark Twain National Forest in southern Missouri. LIES AND LUST NOW was followed, two miles down, by TORMENT FOREVER. The message concluded another two miles along. REPENT! In each instance, the words were superimposed on an American flag. This singular sequence of twenty-foot-tall signs was wildly outnumbered by the postings of individual, if indistinct, merchants: GIRLS GUNS LIQUOR LOANS.

The last stretch of road to Branson was under construction. Blasting was in progress to make room for more lanes. Flashing beacons slowed the traffic, guiding us around machinery and mounds of boulders, but due to wet conditions, no one was on site.

For a couple of minutes, the RV in the adjacent southbound lane matched the bus's speed. The driver of the motorhome was parallel to me as we all eased through the slow zone. He was wearing half-moon bifocals; his head was tipped back, and his nose was scrunched up. He seemed to be studying the road as if it was a fossil and he was an archeologist. Then he shook his head, as though having failed to identify the life form, and he began to speak. A woman, crowned with a falsely brown perm, popped into the space at his right and handed him a sandwich.

— Hot mustard, honey? —No thanks, dear. Don't forget my heartburn.

The man took a tentative bite. Then, in order to get a better grip on the sandwich, he briefly let go of the steering wheel.

The bus driver found an opening and we pulled ahead.

Early evening, I marched along a glittering stretch of country music venues, cowboy regalia shops, and steakhouses. Parking lots spread with puddles doubled the influence of so many bulbs, so much neon. At first glance, Branson was a stunted cousin to Vegas.

Whatever strangeness the place had to offer could wait. Soon I hoped to be spread on a bed, pacifying the whim for privacy. As a rule, there were cheap motels within walking distance of the bus station (which, in Branson, was a pickup point outside a family restaurant). I was a conscientious shopper, and had learned that if I hoofed it another quarter mile, I could pay $22.99 for the night rather than $26.99 at an establishment offering dubious extras. I knew from experience that "continental breakfast" could mean three coconut donut holes.

I arrived beneath the pink sign of the El Dorado Inn, relieved that its mad blinking hadn't just been a psychedelic mirage. The employee slid the paperwork under the bulletproof shield separating us. I scribbled on the form and pushed it back with cash. I was buying time, the right to lock myself away for some portion of twenty-four hours.

My room was at the rear. A car without licence plates, hubcaps or a future on any road was parked outside my door. This wasn't a great comfort, but the trick with omens was knowing which ones to ignore. I inserted my key, amused by the shaky lock, laughable fodder for a toothless crook. The door itself seemed to be cardboard reinforced by several coats of paint that could easily be kicked in by an angry spouse or a cheated dope hawker.

I shut the world out and settled in quickly. After turning on the one working lamp that bathed everything in jaundice yellow, I flopped on the bed with a three-dollar six-pack of Genesee. A shower could wait. I opened the first can of weak beer and more fully absorbed the faux-wood panelling, the faux-marble sink counter, and the faux sense of security. And I absorbed that now-familiar aroma, a brew of dust, mould, cheap perfume, the body odour of a thousand hard-breathing salesmen, and a million exhalations of smoke. An accumulated stink I was used to.

Even cheap motels were something of a luxury for me. I savoured these chances to relax, to be a dumb lump on a worn queen-sized. I loved the break from sitting on a bus. I could still hear the road, when I listened for it, but in the meantime I was outside of those hasty rhythms.

Eventually I got up to take a peek at the nearby world, parting the brown curtains just an inch. I felt like a holed-up outlaw, although I wasn't entirely sure what crime had been committed, or whether or not I should feel guilty about something. Rather than an athletic bag overflowing with blood-speckled bills or a silver suitcase full of pillowy cocaine, I had stolen freedom, piles and piles of freedom, more freedom than one person could spend in a lifetime. And then I was seized by a recurring feeling of deficiency. Where was the girl, the brassy dame who drove the getaway car? Didn't I need a sexy accomplice?

Motel rooms reminded me that even though I had a lot, I was very much alone.

I cracked another beer and reluctantly admitted emotion to myself, acknowledged a yearning for—what? My ex-girlfriend? A straightforward purpose? Or, in those passing moments, was I just longing for home? A gentle sorrow was my occasional mistress, arriving soundlessly at the thin door of my road-worn spirit. I always let her in, invited her into the wide bed. She never stayed long, only warming me until she trusted I was satisfied. Melancholy was a dependable lover.

There were other ways to circumvent thought, other addictions with which to occupy myself. Oh, here it comes, that's it, H-B-O and E-S-P-N and W-K-R-P, yes, right there, into my E-Y-E-S, into the V-E-I-N-S, geezus gawd, yes.

I made sure I was extremely tired when the TV finally went off; otherwise, the erratic pings of the fan became a form of torture, and the feet walking by outside that always seemed to stop at my door could get me thinking again.

Two days later I was having breakfast at The Golden Corral and considering my options. They were the same as ever. Stay or go. Had I done Branson justice? What better way to kill indecisive time than an all-you-can-eat buffet? I was standing at the self-serve waffle counter, and I must have looked confused. An enormous man came up next to me and poked my arm with a spoon.

"Waffle rookie, huh?" he said. He grinned, and took charge, pouring the correct amount of batter into the iron. "Now just close her up and wait three minutes." He was wheezing. He paused between statements to gather the necessary breath. "All your sauces are over there." Crackling inhalation. "They're real good."

He headed for his table. On his plate a tidy six-sausage pyramid had been constructed next to an expansive dune of scrambled eggs. He was half my height and twice my weight, Humpty before the great fall. I slid into my booth, and spread a paper napkin on my lap. Before I began to eat, I realized my waffle helper was looking at me from three tables over. I lifted my first forkful of syrup-drenched dough with one hand, and gave a thumbs-up with the other. The fat man winked, his jaw gnashing on sausage. His portly wife turned to look at her husband's new buffet pal. She smiled. Her teeth were purple with grape jelly.

Our pitiable gluttony reminded me of Elvis. The previous day I had attended a show of impersonators, among them Mr. Presley, circa a couple years before his ignoble death. When he hit the stage and the lights hit him, the crowd gasped. An acute emotion was passed around instantaneously. The package of details was exact and predictable: the sculpted sideburns, the jumpsuit that would befit no other mortal, the slick chest, the swagger. *It's practically Him, isn't it?* We were within imagining distance.

As part of the encore Elvis kneeled at the front of the stage to kiss a dozen women who had rushed to get in line. He gave them each a red silk scarf moistened with genuine stage sweat. The women walked away holding the souvenir close to their chests, childlike smiles playing on their faces.

After the show a few impersonators lingered to talk with fans. Tina Turner, Bette Midler, Roy Orbison. Unfortunately, Elvis had left the building. Once most of the admirers had dispersed, I chatted with Neil Diamond. Up close the myth was as wax: a face heavy with stage makeup, a comb-over stuck in its billowy place. Did false Neil ever get bored?

"I don't mind," he said. "Every day you have to be convincing all over again."

"Do you get harassed on the street?"

"Sometimes," he said. "People think celebrities look slightly different in person. But ultimately I'm anonymous. When the gig ends I return to my incognito life."

I congratulated Neil on a solid set. He thanked me and went off to wash his face.

The last song of his set had certainly been the most memorable. Four busty backup singers had jogged onto stage dripping in red, white and blue, each waving a large flag. Dry ice vapour had billowed. Cymbals had crashed. A few people near me had sung along. "We huddle close. Hang on to a dream. On the boats and on the planes, they're coming to America…"

The waffle experiment a success, I acquired a plate of eggs and hash browns. While chewing, I read the rules of dining in the plastic mini-menu holder (buffetiquette). The first line seemed strange: *Feel free to return for a second portion of items you particularly enjoyed.* I thought that was the whole idea. *The manager may restrict repeated servings of certain items or unusually large portions.* Fair enough. *For the safety of children please help them at the buffet.* Yes, please, think of the children. They knew not what they were headed for: swollen ankles, blown knees, heart disease at forty.

Youth, however, was scant in Branson. Most of the coifs around town were silver and permanent. Most of the cars in the lots were long and wide. Branson was a mecca for the aged. At the Acrobats of China show, for example, I was the youngest audience member by at least twenty years. Antacids were available at the snack bar, hearing aids and timeshares advertised in the show program. As part of one act a girl lying on her stomach slowly brought her legs over her head until her feet were touching the ground in front of her eyes. The man sitting nearest me in the darkened auditorium groaned. "My back hurts just lookin' at that!" We *ooh*-ed at the Thrilling Nose Balance and Death-defying Double Poles. We *aah*-ed at the majestic architecture of eight people riding on a single-seat bicycle. We suspended our disbelief that standing at the top of a fifteen-foot tall stack of chairs was a skill derived from village peasants.

Again, the performers came to the lobby after the show, standing in a line to accept praise. For many of the idling grandparents, an eleven-year-old girl in a white and silver tutu was the favourite. Her lips were blood red, her cheeks pink, her eyelashes curled and dark. "Simply a darling," someone said. An eighteen-year-old woman stood behind the girl with a protective hand on her shoulder. Through the group's interpreter, I talked to the elder girl. She had spent her Beijing childhood perfecting the ability to balance full champagne glasses on various parts of her head and face.

"What do you think of America?" I asked.

"Better."

"Better than China?"

"Better weather."

"Would you like to live here?"

"I hope to learn the culture."

"How do you entertain yourselves?"

"E-mail to home."

I assumed their time between performances was passed reclusively in one of Branson's motels, living the sequestered existence of the visitor. Not unlike what I had been doing.

Rain was imparting a gloomy eternity on the young day. Though peculiar and distracting, Branson was a one-note town: entertainment. I thought I had taken a fair sample. (I went to see the impersonators as something of a fake; the marketing reps from both shows were thrilled to accommodate a Canadian journalist.) The once-daily southbound bus didn't get in until 6:00 p.m. I got to The Golden Corral at 10:00; I ate well and slowly. Staff began carrying away stainless steel trays, replacing them with those bearing lunch items. It was noon. The waiter who had been refilling my coffee came over and put a few clean plates on my table.

"I thought you could get some lunch," he said. He nodded at my pack, perched opposite me on the booth. "You're just killing time, right? Waiting for a bus or something?"

"I am, actually."

"Go ahead. Nobody's gonna know."

I went back to the aisles of fresh hot food and loaded up on steamed vegetables and fried chicken. The waiter and I talked as he wiped down nearby tables. He was about my age. He'd grown up in Elkhart, Indiana, where he was anxious to return. All his people were there. "My mom works in Branson," he said. "She dragged me down here and I haven't been able to leave. I hate it. It's a circus."

The meal lasted until 3:00 in the afternoon. And it would represent all three meals. During the extended proceedings I stashed an apple, a banana and a sticky bun in the top of my pack, items that would suffice as evening snacks. *Help us maintain our reasonable prices by not removing food from the premises.* Alas, it was a rule I had to break. I waved to the kind waiter from the door, and stepped out onto the main drag.

"See our little friend there?" The cabbie was pointing up at a sleek black helicopter. "The feds looking for drugs. The weed is Missoura's biggest cash crop, and it's harvest time."

He lit a cigarette and gazed over the mist-filled valley. Branson's strip was six miles long, and I was at the opposite end from the bus depot. Deciding that a wet, three-hour walk didn't suit my sensibility, I flagged a taxi. The green hills were bathed in grey, like laundry soaking in dirty water. I caught a brief and occasional glimpse of a homestead or two, shrouded apparitions among the faraway trees.

"Hell," said my chauffeur. "It's a good day just to get stoned." He was unshaven and his eyes were pink and wet; he had likely already taken his own advice. "What I would really like is—"

"We got two gals need a ride to Wal-Mart," said the dispatcher. "Who's close to the Good Shepherd Inn?"

"Jesus," said the cabbie. He turned down the volume of his receiver. "Glad I won't be taking that one."

Another helicopter buzzed overhead.

"Okay," he said. He gestured toward the clouds, and waited to catch my eye in the rear-view. "Them white and blue ones is full of tourists. Fifty-some bucks a head. Can you believe people pay to see all this shit from the sky?"

"No," I said.

He nodded. We passed a motel in the shape of a Mississippi paddle wheeler. "Christ," he said, blowing smoke out his slightly open window. "Would you stay in a place like that? I don't think I could sleep. The fuckin' beds around here have held more big old butts than any place in Missoura." Again he focused on me in the mirror. "Can I tell you something?"

"Sure."

"I grew up here, right, when Branson was nothing but a town on a river. If you took me as a kid and dropped me somewhere on the strip today I prob'ly wouldn't know where the fuck I was. This place is a machine, a big ugly machine. I guess machines is supposed to get bigger and uglier." Some of the other afternoon shows had ended and a traffic jam was forming before our eyes. The driver snorted. "Not only do we got twice as many cars as will fit, everyone insists on driving twenty miles an hour." He flicked his cigarette butt out the window. "Seven million people every year," he said. "You know that?"

I shook my head. Two members of that seven million were standing on the sidewalk beside the cab as we sat in traffic. They were holding bulky, awkward bags. They looked up the strip, and then down, and then up again. They looked lost. The driver snorted again. "Ain't these old gals a laugh? Them purses always got more money."

We passed the venues for Buck Trent, Mickey Gilley, and Moe Bandy, their billboard mugs framed by a thousand light bulbs. The names meant little to me, although I was oddly pleased to attach a face to the artist known as Tony Orlando. His hair was a gelled black helmet, his moustache a chunky slug; he oozed suave.

"Do you go to any shows?" I asked, seeking the outrage.

"Fuck, no," he said. "I ain't into has-beens." He laughed and coughed. "This is the hell of country music. After your career dies, you go to Branson to make a shitload of money. They say Jim Stafford's bin doing the same jokes, to the word, for the last eight years. The fucker's just sittin' at the teat—"

Another cabbie interrupted him. "I can't take that Wal-Mart call," said a crackling voice. "I gotta get my granddaughter from school. She's got nits in her hair again."

"Nits," I said, almost by accident.

"Sure," said my driver. "She's a real hick place underneath."

The cabbie got out with me at the depot. He lifted my backpack from his trunk, holding it up while I eased my arms through the shoulder straps.

"Awright, bud," he said. "Good luck goan."

I waited for the Little Rock bus beside a father and daughter. When I dropped my pack she looked down at it, then up at me. "Where you goan?" she said.

"Memphis, I think," I said.

"Memphis, Arkinsas?"

Her father cut in. "Memphis, Tennessee," he said. "Ain't no Memphis in Arkinsas. You needa learn yer history." He flicked his head at me. "Watch yerself at the station down there. They'll be on ya right away."

"Who?" said his daughter for both of us.

"Them niggers. Lookin' for dimes. They's why we left and come here."

It suddenly seemed improbable that I had made it all the way to Branson without meeting a bigot. I cleared my throat, said nothing. No one wants to be told they inspire feelings of brutal disappointment.

23

A black man with a limp approached me at the station in Little Rock. He was lugging a transparent garbage bag of folded clothing.

"What size pants you wear?" he said.

Fatigued, lost in thought, and unaccustomed to being asked that question by anyone other than my mother, I stared at him blankly.

"What size?" he said. "C'mon, man. Let me show you what I got."

My half-hearted wave sent him along to the next customer. I realized gradually that more than a few people wore matching dark blue jeans with bright yellow stitching.

I sat up, rotating soreness along the length of my spine. I was waiting for the 1:00 a.m. to Memphis, and midnight was being shy. *Express*, they called the short haul route on I-40. I would rather the ride lasted till dawn. Sleeping on the bus was a way to save a buck, but one had to plan carefully in order to get a solid six-hour rest. Shuffling in and out of rooms populated by the rundown and somehow sorry was a tired purgatory.

A man was napping under the row of metal chairs across from me. His back was cushioned by drugstore flyers, his feet wrapped up in the business pages. Swaddled in garbage, he found comfort. A security guard who had passed several times eventually decided to address the situation. He nudged the guy softly with a shiny black boot, checking for life. The man groaned, coughed, rolled out from beneath the chairs, and struggled to stand. He was human driftwood, washing on and off the beach of the streets at irregular intervals. He grunted what I assumed was a request to use the washroom, where he stayed for the worst part of the next hour; the security guard went to find other ways to tick off the time left on his shift.

I told myself that station hours were a personal challenge, an endurance test. Try not to eye the clock. Try not to sigh. Try to exercise a little faith. Perhaps waiting was part of heaven's payment schedule: *Free rides to the sandcastle in the sky for those who demonstrate patience!* It was best to believe that no matter how many hours remained before departure there was *not enough time* to understand the immediate universe. The diversion of people was always near, and often chaotic. I resolved to pop tedium like a seedpod, to find poetry in the ordinary. I just had to close my eyes for a moment.

I woke sweaty and bothered in the Sycamore View Motel three miles from downtown Memphis. When I turned on the TV, the lunchtime news anchor's big head told me that a man who had been shot last night died later in hospital. Police had no suspects. Kicking off the sheets, I walked outside barefoot. The Mississippi River could be seen from the second-floor landing, a piecemeal movement of brown beyond the trees. I breathed in deeply. It was late October and *hot*. I didn't know where the South officially began, but for me it had just started.

What now, then? If this was a new chapter, I should hit the bricks running. Throw myself into an oncoming occurrence. Talk to a cop or a junkie; better yet, get them both at once, the tired two-way ire when neither would be listening. I had a cold shower and brewed a pot of vile motel coffee. I sat on the edge of the bed, slumped toward the small screen. *Sinkhole stops traffic on Macon Cove*: images of puzzled motorists and emergency personnel. I turned off the TV and got dressed. My usual loose ends lacked their usual consolation. Aimlessness, at times, could be a bother. While the hopeful wander guaranteed one result or another, so did asking for a recommendation. Down fractured concrete steps I went to the lobby. The manager who had checked me in three hours earlier was still on duty.

"You wanna see something, but you don't wanna be the tourist," he said.

I couldn't have put it more succinctly. He said he was heading into the city, and could drop me off. There was someone I might like to meet.

Jacqueline Smith had only vague memories of when Martin Luther King Jr. was assassinated.

"There was a curfew, so we couldn't go outside," she said. "The city was on fire."

Jacqueline lived on the sidewalk across the street from the Lorraine Motel, where King was shot to death in 1968. She was a longtime protester of the National Civil Rights Museum, built adjacent to the Lorraine so that its balcony could be used as the central exhibit. A couple of period cars were purchased and parked beneath a wreath that was affixed to the railing of the second floor, where King collapsed.

"They spent $9 million to glorify a building of empty, unused rooms," said Jacqueline. She'd moved into the Lorraine a few years after the assassination and become one of many permanent residents. Eventually, city officials decided that the site would make a decent tourist attraction, and Jacqueline was evicted with the other tenants, physically removed from the room that had been her home for sixteen years.

Home became a shopping cart brimming with books, clothing and various food items. A stack of cardboard and plastic sheeting was folded nearby in case of inclement weather. She stayed in place rain or shine, with an umbrella to deflect either, and slept on a dirty white couch.

Jacqueline was petite with a hive-like hairdo, and she sat up straight, birdlike and graceful. Hers was a passive passion. As we talked, she gazed over my shoulder at the vacant motel.

"The Lorraine sits as a memorial to one violent moment," she said. "The museum wasn't set up for the purposes of helping anyone. The whole deal is a sham. A shame."

She didn't sound angry, just quietly frustrated. Between comments she flipped idly through the weekend papers. Although the museum was closed for Sunday, at three- or four-minute intervals a curious carful pulled over on the opposite curb and jumped out to get a picture of the site.

"The motel room door where a man was shot dead," she said. "Why would you want a photo of that?"

The people would eventually look over and slowly absorb the sentiment of Jacqueline and her signs. BOYCOTT THE MUSEUM. TOURIST SCAM. Some waved apprehensively. Those who crossed the street were greeted by Jacqueline and handed a copy of King's final sermon, a few lines of which were on a banner draped over the cement wall behind her. *I did try to feed the hungry, I did try to clothe the naked, I tried to love and serve humanity.*

I met Jacqueline on day 286 of year twelve of her protest. She had a dream that the infamous motel would become a free community college, a health clinic, affordable housing, anything but a tacky tribute to a national scar.

"I'll be here until his memory is put to better use," she said. "Until we respond to his words." She looked down at the newspaper in her lap, which was opened to a photo spread of holiday trends. "I'll be here as long as it takes."

The second tip from the motel manager involved an Elvis fanatic in Mississippi, a man who apparently was in the process of transforming his home into a replica of Graceland. Unsure of the specifics, the manager directed me to Shangri La Records on Madison Avenue in midtown Memphis. He said they would know what I wanted to know.

It was a long walk to Shangri La. On the way, I saw a Cadillac get rear-ended. No one shook a fist. No one asked me to remain as a witness. I saw boarded-up storefronts and advertisements that said *advertise here!* I saw a man, naked from the waist up, blowing smoke out a broken window. I saw, next to the merry-go-round at a vacant playground, a weather-beaten porn magazine. Folded open to a blow job. (I had leaned on the peeling white fence for a closer look.) I crossed a vast and mostly empty parking lot punched through with weeds, and entered the Piggly Wiggly, hunting for sustenance. A produce manager in a Mr. Pig apron directed me to the grocery's cafeteria, where I acquired a container of bean salad and sat down next to a woman whose heavy breasts were striped with veins, and who was passing a bottle of formula back and forth between jittery twins. I saw that a third child, being old enough to chew, was eating fried chicken. Happily.

Shangri La wasn't far from the Piggly Wiggly. The clerk at the record store didn't need many clues as to my search. "It's called Graceland Too," he said. "I went down there myself once. It's strange." I looked at him, wanting more. "You know," he said. "*Strange.*" He provided me with the home address of one Paul B. MacLeod, and I suddenly had a date in Holly Springs, Mississippi.

At a transit bus stop, as I waited for a lift back downtown, I thought back to Graceland itself. I had gone to see the real thing the previous afternoon. I went, in part, because it was free. From my room at the Sycamore View, I had called the Media Relations Department, told a helpful man that I was a freelancer from Canada working on a story about things to do for fun in Tennessee. He didn't mind that I couldn't say when, or in what publication, the story might appear: a complimentary pass would be waiting for me at the Special Services counter.

I had been immediately relieved not to have paid to be part of the spectacle. With doe-eyed adults and confused kids, I was herded through the mansion. On a portable cassette player, each of us had Priscilla Presley's voice as accompaniment. We saw the piano, the pool table, the toaster, the furniture and televisions. In the backyard, I watched as a woman snatched a leaf from the ground and slipped it into her brochure.

Graceland was a curiosity, but I was unable to see it as much more than a crowded display of common and bland religion. (Elvis, like Jesus, was an individual who had become an industry.) And although I had accepted that my trip was, in part, a gathering of eccentrics and oddball devotees, I wasn't prepared to contend with *so many* of them—thus my interest in Paul B. MacLeod.

I also realized the trend was continuing whereby I was going out of my way to find people who were out of the ordinary. But how could I go out of my way? There *was* no way until I went. Holly Springs would be the next stop in a series of detours.

Who should walk up and take the spot next to me on that midtown bench but a Greyhound driver? We sat in silence for fifteen minutes, watching the Friday night traffic honk its way toward the city. The man beside me started knocking the heels of his black shoes together.

"Somebody's dragging his feet," he said. "Spinning the wheels. Spending my time." The irony wasn't lost on him. "If I'm late, the bus I got to drive will be late, and that many more people get angry. It starts right here."

The bench was in front of a fire station. All three of the building's tall garage doors were raised, all emergency vehicles—two red fire trucks and one yellow ambulance—accounted for.

"Any time now a truck will come racing out of there," he said, gesturing behind us. "I know this neighbourhood, and this neighbourhood knows the sound of sirens."

The driver was soft-spoken and handsome, and had a salt-shake of grey on each side of a neatly sculpted afro. A suit bag was draped across his lap and a duffel bag was on the ground. He said he was the night shift guy who usually took a bus to Nashville and back or one to Jackson and back.

"Driving a bus isn't like trucking where you're out fourteen days at a time. Most weeks I'm in my own bed every night." That night he was on his way to Little Rock. To accommodate his mother-in-law's funeral, he had switched shifts with another driver. "Unfortunate that we lost her, but fortunate also, you know," he said. "At least I can be there. I'll take a bus out, pay my respects, and bring a busload back." He yawned. "I'll tell you what the toughest thing is: when you get thirty miles out of the city and you're surrounded by darkness and the sleep starts closing in." He shrugged. "They give us a few tips. One is to keep your eyeballs moving," he said and illustrated for me, looking up, left and right quickly as if tracking a hummingbird. "That's the main one. Take everything in, as many details as possible. Don't start staring at anything in particular. I also tap my feet, move my head, shake my shoulders—people look at you like you're a fool—but it helps to get a rhythm going. Then all you do is keep changing the rhythm."

From inside the fire station behind us, an intercom crackled loudly to life. *Fifteen-year-old…chest pains…forty-five minutes…* We turned to see two attendants enter from the back of the station and slip into the cube ambulance. They pulled out to the sidewalk and wailed a warning to the traffic. Our downtown bus was finally in view, rolling to a stop at the rear of a long line of yielding cars.

The driver stood and hoisted his two bags. "Bottom line is, you got to stay aware."

Quickly counting the quarters in my palm, I stepped into the bus behind him.

24

Paul B. MacLeod was groggy when he finally answered the door to his antebellum mansion in Holly Springs. His thinning black hair was tousled, his eyes moist and half-closed. "Come on in," he said.

I stepped inside.

"I'll be right back."

Looking around in the lobby area I became a little concerned that I hadn't told anyone where I was going that day. Every inch of wall and ceiling space was taken up with posters, newspaper clippings, records, and magazine covers, and the stairway was clogged with toys and dolls, a thousand Elvis eyes frozen in place, watching.

When he returned a few minutes later, Paul's hair was greased to a shine and combed back, and his sizable sideburns were flattened and trim. I caught a whiff of aftershave.

"Okay, here we go," he said. "The greatest private collection of Elvis material in the world." He waved me into the next room. The ceiling was papered with large sheets of playing cards sealed in protective plastic. He saw me looking up.

"Bought 'em for one cent, each is worth $5,000 now, they were worth that much the instant Elvis died. Over here you got square-inch chunks of carpet from the original jungle room, these could get me millions in no time on the Home Shopping Network. See this record? *TV Guide Presents Elvis*, only fifteen copies made, it's the most valuable record in the world, I could trade it in tomorrow for a gold Rolls Royce. Right here you got some of the first flowers left at the gravesite. I was there."

He handed me a clear plastic bag full of brown stems and crushed petals. Paul gave his spiel like an auctioneer, talking so fast that spit gathered at the corners of his mouth. At regular intervals he plowed the white bubbles away with his left hand while his right hand pointed to the next item on the block.

I followed him deeper into the house. The next room was lined with large trunks stacked three high that contained 30,000 videotapes—"in mint condition"—of film and television references to Elvis, all precisely catalogued. Four TVs sat in a row flickering to four different stations, and each had an adjacent VCR so as many mentions as possible were captured.

"In the last twenty-four hours there's bin 106 mentions of Elvis," he said. "That's about average."

Although smaller and more cramped, the space was disturbingly and intentionally similar to the basement at Graceland where Elvis would watch numerous programs simultaneously. I noticed a messy blanket-covered couch, and realized Paul B. MacLeod had been sleeping next to these competing televisions and hadn't heard me knocking. Then my eyes were drawn to the far wall, to the shrine's radiant epicentre: a giant portrait of the young and handsome Elvis adorned with a string of coloured lights and framed on one side by a reminder of time gone since the man's premature demise. 23 YEARS IS FOREVER.

"More people watched *Aloha From Hawaii* than were watching when man landed on the moon."

Paul looked me in the eyes, wanting to make sure I believed him, though I don't know who would have doubted his zeal. Other clues suggested his fervour was real. For example, he had named his son Elvis Aaron Presley MacLeod. Randomly interspersed within the wall collage was a history of Paul's own Elvis. There he was in the bathtub as an infant, in the backyard with a baseball bat, wearing a tie and gown at graduation.

"Ain't he just the spitting image?" said Paul.

Elvis MacLeod was a thinner, taller version of his dad. I avoided eye contact with Paul. "Who's that?" I asked, pointing at another shot.

"That's my wife in the back of a Caddy."

"What happened to her?"

"Eventually she said 'Elvis or me?' and I said Elvis. I didn't have to think for long."

Paul had grown up in Michigan and, unsurprisingly, used to work on a Cadillac assembly line. He grabbed my arm, quickly forgetting about his former life and lesser love.

"Here," he said. "See if I can't get close to His voice for the hell of it. I got this strep throat but we'll see."

He coughed, tilted his head toward me and eventually let loose with a ragged verse of "All Shook Up." As a follow-up he lifted a pant leg and mimicked the Elvis shake. He was becoming more buoyant as the tour progressed.

In Paul's version of the record room, worn forty-fives were hanging from the wall like loose tiles. "Every single that Elvis ever released is here, and some he didn't," he said. "It's a damn near priceless collection."

That Paul would ever trim his collection for profit seemed unlikely. The fact that he could—and for millions, apparently—was what mattered, proof to visitors that his faith was legitimate.

In Graceland Too's pseudo-jungle room, where swaths of shag carpet had been nailed to the walls, Paul displayed the photo of every person who had taken his tour. They were posted on massive sheets of cardboard, hundreds of faces per sheet. He estimated about 200,000 had passed through so far. Each, including me, was photographed below the portrait shrine, many smiling uncertainly. As I stood in the narrow room with all those tiny eyes looking out at me, tiny thumbs raised or hands waving, and my host waiting in silent dimness at the opposite end, I didn't know whether to laugh or scream or hide my face until the dream broke. Then Paul removed from the wall what looked like a shotgun. Apropos of what, I had no idea. I couldn't recall if Graceland had a munitions room. Paul bounced the weapon in his hands, relishing its heft.

"I could drop an elephant at 1,000 yards," he said.

My uneasy mind raced back through the rooms we had seen and out the door, onto a shady street of Holly Springs, which was a war-statue town in Mississippi, which was a state but also a river that nearly dissected the entire union of America, which was a chaotic construction of spare parts assembled hastily by a mad genius. Outrageous and mesmerizing, America was art.

"Quite a home you have here," I said.

Paul nodded. He returned the gun to its rack, and became ebullient again. "I'm surprised five people haven't knocked on the door while I bin talking to you," he said. "You wouldn't believe the limos that stop out front, girls in hot tubs, midgets serving drinks. I got a Utah station coming next week. We bin mentioned in books. People say my story should be its own book, that if it was made into a movie it would sweep the Academy Awards. Do you know anyone in the publishing world, in the film world? There's money to be made."

I edged toward the front door, wanting away from this salesman who was offering his own mania at such a discount. He kept talking as I pulled on my pack.

"Graceland Too is known all over the country," he said. "All over the world."

The timing was poor to tell him how only one of the two gas station attendants I talked to a mile away had ever heard of his house. "Something to do with Elvis," she said. "Yeah. I ain't never bin there." Nor was she able to provide directions.

Paul watched from the front door when I left. When I got to the sidewalk, he called to me.

"Send your friends to see me," he said.

I nodded, and started off down the empty street. I had been hoping Paul B. MacLeod would be worth at least fifteen minutes of my time. I ended up giving him and his slanted house an hour and a half.

"All right?" he said, louder.

I turned.

"Send them down," he said.

"I will," I called.

I went back to the gas bar where the Greyhound paused while in Holly Springs. The southeasterly run that had dropped me off earlier wouldn't pass through again until the next day. However, the northwesterly route was scheduled to arrive in an hour. I would return to Memphis, then head south to Jackson.

25

We were somewhere north of Jackson when the wheels stopped turning. The driver steered us onto the shoulder and switched on the strip of overhead lights, both harsh interruptions of the night ride. I had almost convinced myself that I was asleep.

Peculiar sounds reverberate along the innards of a bus. Sometimes the voices I thought were in my head were coming from the mouths of people in front of or behind me. The brain does its best to find something consistent to latch onto: the steady hum of tires on concrete, the engine's low rumble, the constant breath of the fan.

Two guys, or maybe more, had been talking energetically for several minutes, spitting a little colourful language into the shadowy guts of the bus. I heard a "cocksucker" or two, a "sonavabitch," and at least one "Jesus fuckin' Christ!"

The swearing stopped when the bus stopped. A few dozing riders groaned and stirred in reaction to the intrusive light. The driver stood and turned to face us. He was wearing a short-sleeved uniform shirt.

His forearms were dark and hairless, and twice the thickness of my own.

"Awright, listen here," he said. "We're gonna dock this ship right now. When we started out, I went over the rules with ya slowly: no drinkin', no smokin', no extra noise. There's one thing I guess I wasn't clear on. No cussin'! There'll be no cussin' on my bus. I don't hardly believe what I bin hearin' up here."

He leaned over and pulled a book out from behind his seat. Then he flipped to one of the many pages marked with a paper tab. I sat up and stole a quick look toward the back of the bus. Many eyes faced forward, peering over the backs of seats curiously. The mood was silent, apprehensive. The driver stepped forward past the first few pews of passengers.

"Now," he said. "I'm gonna share some little wisdom with ya. Maybe ya don't know about how Moses was called up the mountain by the Lord, but I know y'all heard about the Ten Commandments before."

To my weary amazement, he kneeled, opened the good book (maroon leatherette, well-thumbed), and cleared his throat.

"Exodus, chapter twenty, verse seven. 'You shall not take the name of the Lord your God in vain; for the Lord will not hold him guiltless who takes his name in vain.'"

Two white-haired ladies were sitting across from me, their hands folded neatly in their laps. Both were wearing soft purple hats and large eyeglasses. As the drama played out, one leaned forward a little and looked down, while the other stared out the window into the darkness, their poise and dignity so far intact.

With his eyes closed the driver was carrying on. "And the people were afraid and trembled, and Moses said to the people—"

"Shut the fuck up! I'm tryin' to get some fuckin' sleep!"

The driver scrambled to his feet. "Who said that?" He took a few steps forward, and was standing almost beside me, his eyes attentive with anger. "Who said that?"

I heard two coughs and a muffled giggle, the sounds of a conspiracy of silence. The usual classroom standoff ensued.

Accomplices won't squeal on the guilty individual and the teacher either has to give up the manhunt or punish everyone. But mass discipline had no possible application this time, and the driver knew it. He had lost long ago, even before bending to the Bible. As the driver cast his eyes around at the innocents among us his frustration receded. "Somebody owes you good folks an apology."

Then a calm, hopeful voice rose from the front seats, behind the driver. "Maybe we should just keep going?"

The driver looked down at his shiny black shoes. "Just felt like testin' me, huh," he said quietly, almost to himself.

He turned around and went back to his controls. Seconds later the overhead lights clicked off and we were once again accelerating south. I glanced behind me over the seat and noticed a couple of people were flopped open-mouthed against their crumpled jackets. Would they believe the story if I related it to them tomorrow? Anyone who was half awake must have learned at least one thing. In the chill dark of a Mississippi roadside long after midnight, a preacher is wise to keep the sermon short.

26

A hostel is just a hotel with a couple of twists. One grimy shower is everyone's property, and the bedroom can resemble an army barracks: bunks in a row on which rest meagre toiletries and unfinished letters home, young men lounging, playing cards and rubbing their skulls.

I entered my assigned room at the Longpré Guesthouse in New Orleans to the sight of a lanky Japanese guy in his underwear doing squats. He hurried to don jeans and a T-shirt, and then greeted me with a nod. I propped my pack against the wall and sat on an empty bottom bed, the last vacancy of three sets of bunks. On one of the top cots, someone was sleeping, or trying to, his naked back facing out.

According to his bilingual business card, Ebiyoshi was a silkscreen artist from Tokyo; he was in town for a conference of similar talents. He said to pronounce his name "A-B," which seemed appropriate considering his limited English.

"*O-hai-o*," he said quietly. "Good morning, Japan. Ohio."

"*O-hai-o*," I said.

"Like in America, Ohio. Easy for you." After finding out where I was from, he practised some of his known vocabulary. "Japan, four season: winter, spring, summer, fall. Canada, cold?"

"Yes," I said, lacking the energy to expound. Stereotype was uncluttered. "Cold and snow," I added.

"Yes," he said. "I will visit in fu-chaw." A muffled snore came from the top bunk. A-B put on his shoes as I took mine off. After the overnighter from Tennessee I wanted to have a short nap and convalesce. My new pal waved from the door.

"Sayonara," I said.

"Yes, sayonara," he said with a grin. "This is good for you."

I lay down and eased my head back into a hammock of intertwined hands. Watched sparse dust float through a prism cast by the morning sun. The bunk beds were pushed up against three of the walls in a U-shape, and a large window took up most of the fourth side. Corner posts were hung with thrown clothes. I closed my eyes and listened to water dripping somewhere deep inside the 150-year-old house.

A few minutes later, a long and lean black guy came in wearing only shorts and a pair of flip-flops and carrying a towel. Dwight's was the bunk above mine and, having just showered, he finished drying himself off as we introduced ourselves.

"Just got here, huh?" he said. "Welcome aboard. Gonna stay a while?"

"Probably a few days."

"That's it? A lot of people who come here don't manage to leave. I don't know if New Orleans is a spider web or a fish net or what it is, but they don't leave. It's called The Big Easy, right? You start relaxin' and keep on relaxin'."

"Is that what you're doing here?"

"Actually, you know what, not me, man, not right now, but everyone else is. No. I got a job these days."

Dwight was in the car-wash business. His work supplies were in a large cardboard box on the floor at the head of the bed: rags, wax, window cleaner, and an electric polisher. "For the finishing touch," he said, holding up the foam-headed appliance. "After I'm done with this baby, the car shines like a star." His smile showed he was missing an eyetooth. He dressed quickly and filled a knapsack with the necessary items. Then he was gone.

Some hours later, I woke, my mouth dry and my body sweaty. I hadn't thought to undress. I crossed the room and looked out on the back patio area. A wire spiral adorned with razor-sharp metal teeth at four-inch intervals topped the perimeter fence, like an oversized slinky stretched out. Three other guesthouse residents were sitting around a table in the courtyard. A fourth chair was empty. There were glasses and bottles on the table. I went outside to park with them under what looked like 3:00 sunlight.

"*Tu parle français?*" said one when he found out I was from Canada.

"*Un peu*," I said. "*Mais, c'est très difficile.*" These were my usual standby lines, which I always hoped would earn me a modicum of respect. *At least he tried.*

"This is Canada for you," he said, nodding gravely. "You see, the problem is simple: communication is not possible. We can't talk to each other. We can say 'John is a boy' or 'I like my dog' but *c'est tout.* How do I say, it never gets off the first floor. *Oui?*"

"*Oui*," I said.

"We cannot get to know a person, he cannot get to know us. This is the challenge. Do I want to be Canadian? Yes, of course. My English is not very good, but I want my Rocky Mountains and the North and the Maritimes, all of this. But I tell you, I think in ten or twenty years Quebec will separate. The young people are very rah rah; they are emotional but not educated; they tell you they would separate but they don't know who to vote for, they only understand one thing: they speak French and most Canadians don't."

"Fuckin' 'ell," said a long-haired Irishman. "If it's not religion, it's language or culture. Everyone wants their own country, their own fuckin' pot to piss on."

"To piss *in*, mate," said the man across from me, an Australian.

"Wha'?"

"Ya piss *in* the pot."

"Wha'ever. Piss all over the pot." The others laughed.

"Same problem in Ireland, *oui?*" said the francophone.

"Christ, yeah, only worse," said the Irishman. "Canadians don't throw stones at each other."

The Australian looked at me. "Would the English Canadian fancy a drink?" From the communal kitchen adjoining the patio he fetched some ice and another glass. Four cups were raised, and I became a recognized member of the party. Whiskey was the lubricant of international unity.

I was no stranger to the society of stragglers. The New Orleans guesthouse was immediately a familiar scene featuring a familiar cast. In dozens of shelters on a handful of continents I had met individuals from various places who were staying for varying lengths of time. Some were privileged offspring living on a shoestring, delaying a return to work or study or yet more uncertainty. Others toiled at tolerable jobs as a way to live where they were for now. I suspected my bunkmate Dwight was one of those. Still others were working as a way to move on. The Australian, for example, had his butchering papers. His plan was to butcher in California. Then he thought he might butcher in B.C. Then he'd go up to Alaska, butcher there for a stretch. The ability to fashion attractive steak was his ticket around the world. While in the city, some of us would tour actively, sampling local cuisine (oysters Rockefeller, crayfish bisque, the po' boy sandwich) between visits to local sites (the Confederate Museum, the French Quarter, the aboveground crypts and vaults of the cemeteries built on mud). Others would focus on idling, attempting to *not* think of home, where staleness was a threat, where demand tended to linger, where a person resided while striving to remain competent in one discipline or another. We were all stowaways, self-exiled from expectation.

The only difference of note between hostels in Thailand, India, Greece, and the U.S. was water quality, though, in general, what dribbled from the tap wasn't to be trusted—thus, in part, the favouring of alcohol. After my first few drinks in that courtyard, I knew considerable portions of my time in The Big Easy would be spent sitting among men who were varieties of me. (At that particular establishment there was only one female resident, a cheerful Mexican who used beer as suntan oil.) Each of us was taking an intermission from the pursuit of much. All of us were living briefly where we had no history.

Days of obligatory observation served to excuse lackadaisical nights. Despite the abundance of protective fencing (and its high-crime reputation), New Orleans appeared more laid-back than on guard. Many of the cars rolling by were long and close to the ground. Young and old alike ambled as though trying to delay arrival. Even the foliage was nonchalant, the live oak branches hanging low and spread wide, tentacles of leaves reaching out casually. Spanish moss dangled like toddler snot.

Walking toward downtown from the Garden District, I passed beneath an interstate connector. Someone had built a place to live on the concrete foundation that sloped up and away from the sidewalk. Within a border of kicked-away trash were makeshift beds made out of wide, rubbery leaves. A garish purple quilt was furrowed next to one of these nests. The shock of discordant colour was, to my eye, a king's cape first, then a pauper's blanket. Eighteen-wheelers shuddered overhead. No one was home.

The afternoon was overcast and gusty: a suggestion to keep moving. The city core was soon in sight.

"Can I get some help, please?"

I was gaining on the man walking in front of me. He was tapping the pavement with a white cane, divining the next curb.

"Can I get some help, please?"

I realized he was calling out to anyone who could hear him, and I was the only one nearby.

"Can I get some help, please?"

"What are you looking for?" I said when I caught up.

He took hold of my arm at the elbow. "There's a music store at 432," he said. I regretted having asked what he was *looking* for, but I assumed he was used to that, looking as in trying to find. I scanned above the storefronts. We were at 540.

"We're pretty close," I said.

"I know. I just need a little help finding the door." I wondered if he could hear sounds from the shop already, or if he somehow felt the rhythm in the sidewalk as we moved along. The glass door of 432 was propped open with a piece of wood. It was an old record store. About ten people were scattered along the rows flipping through used vinyl.

I slowed to a stop. "There's a step," I said.

The blind man let go of my arm and slipped through the door without a word. I closed my eyes for a few seconds, and next to the music of traffic I was able to hear some jazz.

I found a man by the name of Mark Anthony Moore playing his trumpet on Canal Street not far from Bourbon. He was sitting on an overturned milk crate below a tree that had sprouted next to the sidewalk. One of his sneakered feet was stretched forward, tapping the beat. I stood nearby and waited for him to finish the tune.

"How's life today?" I asked.

"I ain't goan worry about it," he said. "But these clouds comin' on hurt the mood. Clouds don't make for a listenin' crowd. They busy havin' themselves a bad aftanoon."

Mark was a bald and heavy black man with a short grey goatee. The crutches leaning against the tree were his. He had arthritis and gout, he explained. The tree itself was old and scarred, its trunk like the wrinkled leg of a dinosaur; the thick claws of roots had lifted and cracked the surrounding sidewalk squares. Mark started into the next song and was immediately swollen with the effort: billiard ball cheeks, neck veins like tense earthworms. And he was sweating, every tune a workout.

"'Mercy Mercy' by Cannonball," he said. After a few deep breaths he started to sing, gently drumming on one knee with the scratched and tarnished trumpet. "I say my bucket's got a hole in it, my bucket's got a hole in it, it can't carry no beer." Mark paused to tell me he was a harmonica master and self-taught in trumpet. "God gave me abilities, so I use them." Only then did I see the Bible sitting face up on top of his battered leather instrument case.

"Can you imagine doing anything else?" I asked.

"I have imagined," he said. "A man wants to start his own mechanics shop but they won't give him a loan. You got to have money to get money. So I do what I can and what I can do is play music for the folks. It's my contribution and it's honest work. I don't make much, but I earn every dirty penny. Six dollars gets me a bed at the mission, a few more gets me food. I'm fightin' for it today."

I noticed a pair of headphones around his neck. "What are you listening to?"

He tapped the shirt pocket over his heart. "I got Louis Armstrong right here. He's teachin' me a few things."

He half spun the trumpet in his hand, one direction then the other, as he gazed up Canal past Rampart. The two-way flow of people was erratic, a jerky blend of sidesteppers in a hurry, sightseers walking while trying to consult maps, plus all the rest who had nowhere to be anytime soon. Mark shut his eyes on the street scene as if to help visualize some superior picture. Beneath the ominous sky, half-lit apartment towers became harmonicas stood on end, and the domed football stadium was briefly just a soft bubble with a slow leak. Tall buildings filled with short lives, the grandest, soundest structures mostly hollow. Mark opened his eyes and looked down Canal Street toward the waterfront.

"It was real in the old days," he said. "I'm talkin' ten, twenty years back. You could really stretch a buck. Now we got all this shoppin' and gamblin', you might not know where you was. It ain't a city no more. It's just a place people do business. I'm leavin' when I can. Get my seaman's rights again, find me a ship and ship out."

He eased into another tune.

"S'at Louis Armstrong?" said a passerby.

Mark lowered the trumpet and sat up a few inches, his spirit buoyed. "You know it. Ain't he worth a dollar to ya'?"

The guy smiled and kept walking with empty palms out and turned up as though checking for rain.

Moments later the rain came. Heavy drops coloured the concrete one dot at a time. Mark quickly gathered his gear. I gave him a crumpled dollar for his words. He thanked me kindly and hobbled off. The water began to fall hard and fast and was soon louder than the traffic. I started to jog haphazardly with other pedestrians. At the corner of Canal and Bourbon an intersection preacher (soiled white suit, Bible in one hand, pamphlets in the other) had his arms out, his eyes closed and a beatific smile on his face as though he had personally requested the rain from its divine vendors and they were finally delivering.

On my fourth night in town, a slightly adjusted roster held court in the guesthouse yard. A diminutive Scot had replaced my fellow Canadian. And there was a fifth member at the table, a guy from New Jersey who had a handlebar moustache and who claimed to have gotten drunk every day since arriving in New Orleans six months earlier. Funny. Very likely true. He poured himself two inches of Jack Daniel's, and added that much cola.

"I've had it!" said the Irishman. "'Bout time I left this country." He had been commanding the crowd. He had a story to tell. The previous week, he and a buddy had run across the football field as Notre Dame was playing Air Force. They were tackled by an offensive line of security officials and driven from the stadium in a police van.

"Fuckin' 'ell," he said. "Back home the cop would say, 'Wha' yeh doin' here so pissed? Go get somethin' to eat and go to bed. Sober up, for chrissake.' I would never be cuffed and thrown in the wagon back home. Never. Least not for tha'."

He had a patchy two-week beard and heavy eyelids, the look of an exhausted fugitive. It was Saturday and he had to return to South Bend, Indiana, to appear in court on Monday morning. He was bracing himself for the vagaries of the American justice system.

"I'll just get an ear-bashin' and pay a fine," he said. "Though I might have to play the dumb Irish card, yeh know, 'This happens all the time where I come from, sirs.' We didn't know they took her so serious, like with all the alumni in the crowd and how we were stompin' on sacred turf, bloody bullshit like tha', maybe we would have thought again before tearin' across the pitch. Notre Dame won in the end, so wha' the fuck. The fightin' Irish went home happy. The American Irish, anyway."

The Irish hooligan swilled his stiff drink and gave an expression suggesting both pleasure and disgust. The crowd laughed at his folly. His expletive-laced frustration was entertaining, a point of national pride. Rather than loiter in Indiana, he decided to hustle down to Louisiana for the few days he had to spare. Though he had arrived from the North like me, he had taken the train.

"The South is fuckin' savage," he said. "I came down through Mississippi, through Meridian and tha'. Unreal."

I realized that I had traversed the state at night. I hadn't been able to see anything out the window except where the headlights faded into the ditch and partially lit the first bank of trees. I felt a pang of guilt that I hadn't paused. What had I missed?

"I think it was Jackson," he said. "Christ, it looks like bombs have been fallin'. The buildings are stained and scorched. There's black holes for windows, the walls are crumblin', garbage is blowin' around. Wha' the fuck? It was like some hellish idea of the future. Yugoslavia wasn't so devastated. An' the houses in the country, fuckin' hell, like shantytowns or wha'ever, flimsy jobs of cardboard and plywood and scrap metal. Rusted cars piled up in gardens of weeds and old bent trees. The homes look abandoned, but yeh can see tha' people are still livin' there. There's clothes on the line and smoke comin' from the chimney and mama sittin' on the deck. They're squattin' in the past, before electricity and runnin' water. I had to remind myself I was in America. Some poor fuckers out there."

All five of us sipped our drinks. I resisted feeling anxious about what had been neglected. Mississippi for me would boil down to one Elvis nut and one outraged bus driver. I could be satisfied with that; I had to be. The list of places one might like to go was endless and altogether outstripped by the list of places one would never get to. There was no cause to muse about what was missed. Perhaps the liquor and male bonding lent me bravado. I did, however, fancy myself a forward thinker. Part of me was already wondering about Alabama.

I took a recess from the assembly of lushes, and went to the dorm room, well aware that in an hour or so one of them would march up to where I lay, and I would be convinced to join their sloppy advance on a neighbourhood pub. In the meantime, I could pretend to myself that I wanted to sleep well, keep a hangover at bay, as I was beginning to consider getting a bus out of town. Eastward. Florida wasn't far now.

In the bedroom, Dwight the car washer was recovering from ten hours of rubbing chrome.

"Hey," I said. I was suddenly mindful of my drunkenness. "How are things?"

"I worked like a dog today," said Dwight. "Like a dog. Sorry if I say that a lot, man, but no one else is gonna remind me." He had long slim fingers and large hands and passed them over his shaven scalp as if it was a crystal ball. He took a seat on the edge of a bottom bunk and appraised me. "So you just travellin' random or what?" he said.

Either Dwight was especially inquisitive, or I was especially forthright and concise. In any case, I encapsulated my so-called mission.

"Just writin' about your life, huh?" he said. "Shee-it. I've thought about doin' that before. I got stories to tell about people. Some from San Antonio, some from Jacksonville, some from Atlanta, some right here. I bin all over the place collectin' juicy stuff. I know character and I've known some characters. Yeah. But it's all just a play, ain't it? And you and me is just in this scene together. Tell me somethin', if you're gonna write a story about the people you meet, how would you start it?"

"I don't know yet," I said. "You can always just start at the start."

"Yeah, guess so," he said. He stood again, and started dumping the remainder of one of his soap bottles into another like a waitress topping up the ketchup. "Awright. Start at the start. And what would you say?"

"You can only say what you've seen and heard. Tell what happened."

"Yeah, right. You know, I think people would want to read about the shit I've seen. I've known a lot of beautiful people, a lot of ugly ones too. Course, I'd have to go back to school, get my spellin' together, right? Get my grammar down." Flashing a friendly jack-o-lantern smile, he removed his shirt and climbed up on the bed above me.

Dwight was one of a few tenants who were pushing the Longpré's three-week limit. The management liked to rotate its clientele, preferring that no one start thinking of the place as home. Dwight had a few days left to decide on his next move.

"Gonna get my own apartment soon," he said. "Pay once a month, eat when I want and what I want, get a TV and remote control, create a little freedom like that. But I don't know. When I get bored of the race in a place, I gotta go, just gotta leave. Don't know why. Last time I left I went to Arkansas, the next time I think I might get to Minnesota. I bin everywhere. Yeah. I bin all over." He thought about that. "I ain't bin to California. Not California. Not yet."

I could tell Dwight was on his back by the way his skinny right arm was hanging off the bed; it was like a broken branch that hadn't yet fallen from the tree. His hand gestured as he talked, the wrist pivoting, the fingers swaying gently along with each point made as if they were conducting a quiet and private orchestra.

I remembered Lone Wolf, the way he nodded during his roll call of cities, the belief he had been everywhere. "What would you do in California?" I asked Dwight.

"Don't know," he said. "Whatever I got to. You always runnin'·
around in this world, you know, you got to hustle to find a bit of
shelter, clothe yourself, feed yourself, all that." There was a pause. He
was closing in on sleep. "I worked like a dog today," he said. "Like a
damn dog."

Feed yourself. The words called up another memory from Red
Deer, Alberta, back when the trip was but a naive boy. I hadn't forgotten
the dutiful paint job. After the last long day of going up and down the
ladder and slapping a brush against thirsty boards, my stain-spotted
arms had ached. My doctor uncle gave me a couple of painkillers to
help me sleep.

Light was faint in the humid room. I held my wrinkled but soft
white hands in front of my face, and then looked again at Dwight's
hand, dark and limp, laced with thick veins. I suspected he would
become one of my beautiful people. Certainly he was a character I
knew (somewhat). While half of me engaged Dwight as a human
being, the other half treated him like an object of art, fascinated by
his lines and colours, considering always how expertly he could be
drawn on paper.

It stood to reason that painting people was easier than painting
houses (or washing cars).

"Hey, man," said Dwight from above me.

"Yeah?"

"I bin thinkin'. If I wrote that book I know what it'd be called."

"What's that?"

"*How The Rich Keep The Poor Underfoot.* Yeah, I think that would
be it."

I watched the ceiling fan spin, wobbling dangerously at half-
speed. I heard a mouse under the bed nosing its way into my bag of
shelled peanuts. "The title can be a good place to start," I said.

"Yeah, right. It's cuz I was thinkin', you just a master or a servant
in this life. Master or servant, that's all."

Seconds later the hand was hanging motionless and Dwight was
snoring lightly. I began listening to sounds from the courtyard: the

slurred punchlines and laughter, ice cubes clinking into the tumblers of transient men. Our sloth was decadent, I thought. I also heard the ambitious mouse beneath my bunk, a determined hunger chewing through plastic. I fell asleep watching for movement in Dwight's curled fingers.

27

It was discount day at participating McDonald's outlets in the Biloxi region: any sandwich item for ninety-nine cents. There were, however, no sullen single moms pushing appeasing grease toward listless children. The restaurant was nearly empty, and remained so even after ten of us from the bus trundled in. I had sat alone from New Orleans, and wanted to sit alone again. The bus was half full and serene, the mist-hung bayou an ideal backdrop for meditation, for the emptying out of concerns.

I took a corner table (thick plastic, shock yellow), and unwrapped my McChicken (beige disk of meat crowned with four shreds of lettuce and a splotch of mayonnaise). Closing my eyes, I tried to push the words *big-time indigestion* from my mind with the words *small blessing.*

While many around me quickly settled in over their own menu choices, some paused to stare. Not at each other, but outside, through the high windows, through the washed-out night. I recognized the look, had seen it here and there all the way back to Dawson City. Tired truckers had the skill of this expression, quietly hunched over their nth coffees. Pairs of pretty, pruned divorcées had it in those breaths of time when neither was talking. Foursomes of older folks had it too, not trying so hard anymore to think of something to say. Though I sometimes felt a novice, I tried to mimic the gaze.

We trained our flat eyes on the traffic coming, and the traffic going. A sight might pass that we were supposed to see, a sudden clarification or yet more ambiguity. This frozen stare suggested survival was easy but satisfaction elusive, and maybe comfort wasn't contentment after all. Then the smell of deep-fried cheapness wafted up, or we thought to wipe our fingers, or the pie arrived—*Oh, you wanted ice cream, didn't you? I'm sorry.*—and the world was again as it always had been. What we asked for was right under our noses. But for a moment the truth had gone astray. The fixed reality drifted away from everyone as if to allow for a more complete impression.

"I tell you what," said a man's voice.

I looked up. A man in a plaid shirt was sitting two empty tables over. I was the one he intended to tell something to.

"I was with her for eighteen years," he said. "She ups and takes it all, the kids, the car, even my clothes. Everthing I worked for, just took from me. I don't even know where they're at. She could have gone where we come from, cuz I can't go there no more. I got history, fines and other shit. If I went back they'd realize they was lookin' for me, lock me up agin. Once yer face is on the wall. Nah. Ain't nothin' there for me now 'cept a chance to stay for good."

He loudly sucked at what was left of his pop.

"Bin tryin' to start over here, but startin' is slow. First I had to get enough together for some decent clothes. I stayed at the Salvation for the thirty days they give; then I had enough for a week at a motel. But I ain't stayin'. My next twenty bucks is buyin' me a ticket to Mobile, and I'll keep movin' as I have to. I tell you what, you only know what you got when you got nothin'. When it's all bin swiped right off yer back."

He burped and sighed.

"Christ," he said. "It's a good fill for three bucks, ain't it?"

He stood and walked away with his tray of garbage.

28

My spirits were flagging by the time we got to Mobile. Deciding to stay for the night, I wandered from the bus depot back down the highway, toward motels we had passed. I rang a bell at the front desk of one that looked suitably affordable. An older Indian man came out of the office yawning. While he went through the motions of admittance I asked what the difference was between a Super 7 and a Super 8, and, while we were on the subject, a Motel 6? He gave it more thought than I expected.

"We are Super 7," he said. He had offered his best explanation. "Where are you from, sir?"

"Canada," I said. "And you? Originally."

"You have a guess?"

"I'm pretty sure it's India, but where in India?"

His face came to life with a big smile. Then he left the counter area and came around to my side of the Plexiglass. He was about sixty, bald, and wearing slippers, light cotton pants and a white undershirt. With his wife and five children, he had left Bombay for London, where he sold liquor for a few years before they came to the U.S., settling first in Los Angeles and then Mobile.

"America is like everywhere," he said. "Some people good, some people bad. For me, it is hello and goodbye with many Americans, but when foreigners come sometimes we can talk. Like us."

I told him about some of my travels, and when he found out I had been to Bombay his eyes became watery; he hugged me tightly, pushing his mottled scalp against my chest. "You are Canada and I am India," he said. "I am very glad that we can be friends. Quickly we can communicate something to each other." He bubbled on. "Some people in Alabama have never been to Texas. You and I and all these places, we are very lucky in our lives to have moved like this."

A muscular black guy came into the lobby wearing dark sunglasses and a ball cap pulled down. "I need a room for an hour," he said.

The motel manager looked past him to the woman waiting in the car outside. "Okay," he said. "Fifteen dollars."

They exchanged key for cash and the man returned to his vehicle.

"Excuse me," said my new Indian friend. "Why are you travelling alone? Where is your wife?"

"I'm not married."

He frowned. "This is not right. You should not waste time." He took a step back and grabbed his crotch with one hand. "God gave us this for a reason: to create. Everyone must have children. What about girlfriends?"

"I had one for a few years."

"Years!" He shook his head, disappointed. "Love is instant," he said, snapping his fingers and holding them an inch below my nose. "It doesn't take ten hours like your bus to Tallahassee, twenty hours to Miami, whatever. It just happens."

Apparently, instant love could also be a matter of careful negotiation. The Indian's parents had found him a future wife—the daughter of another respectable merchant in Bombay—and introduced the two of them when they felt he was ready. I didn't ask him if he loved her. The question may have given offense, and I wasn't sure I could hide my doubt of what would be an automatic answer. *Of course! Of course! We are* married! Whether or not the relationship was loveless, it had been productive. While four of his five kids were married and spread around the country, the fifth and youngest, his lone boy, was without a mate.

"People have been calling about him, and I say another six months, we'll see. But there will be no courting with the clubs and bars, now holding hands, now kissing, maybe someday family, no, there will be no hussing and fussing. They will meet, go to the restaurant, and have the interview. Questions this way, questions that way, they get to know each other and they decide. Later, there is a tea party."

He said about thirty-five other Indian families lived in Mobile.

"Not many," I suggested.

"Yes, no," he said. "But we have each other. This is advice from me, okay? You should look for a Canadian girl because that is your blood, that is her blood, you will share experience and understanding."

I was in no mood to debate the merits of marriage, intercultural or otherwise. I pleaded fatigue and hunger, neither of which was a lie. Before getting me a room key he insisted on another hug. He shook me gently as he squeezed. We were a pair of citizens-in-absentia from different former British colonies. My passport designation meant instant trust.

"I am glad it was not only check-in, check-out, but we can talk," he said. "We can open our stories. And we will see each other again in the morning."

My unit was three shades of brown, and had twin beds. I threw my pack on one, and collapsed on the other. Soon I sat up, put both pillows behind me, and opened a beer. I wondered vaguely if the motel manager might batter me with his chattiness again tomorrow, and how I might be able to avoid him. He was friendly enough, and I probably should have been flattered that my arrival boosted his spirits, but I resented the certainty of his life counselling. He had practically suggested I modify my thinking, and soon.

What single man in his twenties didn't ask himself now and then whether he might one day be in a partnership that could lead to babies? Everyone was familiar with the inner voice that whispered *multiply*. But I think each of us heard that particular call of nature at a different volume. I remembered again the time I might have walked into a wife and child (or three). That wasn't so long ago. I could have called my ex right then. Talked manically of fresh starts and making it work by working harder and what kind of geography would make us both happy because maybe it wasn't us that was the problem but rather the world we were in. We could have talked about taking another run at the fairytale.

Instead of calling my ex, I called my father. I was overdue to update him on my progress, though it didn't seem as though I had much to report from Mobile. Dad was the one who had news, and quite literally. He had received a piece of mail from Rugby, North Dakota. I had left his Kincardine, Ontario address with the widow, and she had forwarded a copy of the article about me that appeared in *The Pierce County Tribune* the week after I left Rugby.

"There's a photo of a young man in a big hat trying to look agreeable," said Dad. He had to stop chortling before he could read me the headers. "'Traveling novelist,' it says. 'Canadian man gathering input for his writing project.'" said Dad. "Sounds pretty serious."

"Life imitating life that might become art," I said.

"Something like that," said Dad. He went on to read the short note that the widow had included. She wrote that she was glad I had decided to stop in the town where she lived. "You must be doing something right," said Dad. "So what happens next?"

"I guess we'll see how much longer Mobile, Alabama will hold me."

Shortly after our call ended, I turned on the TV. It was 11:30; the day's last local newscast was underway. There had been a car accident on Shell Road near Sage Avenue; a thirty-three-year-old man had been taken to hospital with undisclosed injuries. Traces of a mysterious toxin had been detected in Mobile Bay. The rain that was probable two days from now would, in all likelihood, be followed by sun.

I absorbed information that didn't matter to me, that *couldn't* matter. In my tired and dreamy state, I was pretending that I had first-hand knowledge of the place, that this was the city I woke to every day of my life. I was pretending Mobile was home.

29

For a long-haul truck driver, my seatmate to Tallahassee was a terrible fidget. He worried his hands in his lap, and frequently craned his head in response to passenger noise. *When will that woman stop clearing her throat every twelve seconds? How can someone eat a bag of chips so loudly?* The aisle seat in the middle of a bus wasn't a road orientation Tab understood.

"It doesn't even feel like we're moving," he said. "A fourteen-hour drive is taking me twenty-two."

Tab transported paper, steel, computers, hazardous material—whatever was piled in one place and had been requested somewhere else—and occasionally drove 6,500 miles in a single week. He had left his vehicle behind in Fort Worth in order to "straighten some things up back home" in Jacksonville.

The truck driver was classically intimidating: burly and unshaven and wearing a ball cap tight and low. He could just as easily have been a rogue biker (separated from both motorcycle and gang). I asked him about his typical schedule and discovered that nothing deflated the imagined bully in a man so much as when he described the natural world. He had just made deliveries to Washington and Oregon.

"Beautiful country up there," he said. "Bee-you-tee-full. And the best season to see it in, too. I didn't know colours like that existed on trees. It was awesome." He waved a thumb in front of me, pointing at the window. "Look around you down here and everything's green, and any other time of the year it's the same. I don't know why they call it the Sunshine State when we get thirty, forty inches of rain. I guess people wouldn't come if they called it anything else." He eyed me. "You just visiting?"

"Yeah. I'll head north soon. Florida's the end of the line."

"It's the end of the line all right," he said. He quickly buried that comment and whatever it hinted at. "You know what a manatee is? They're sort of like dolphins, I guess. Big strange animals. They often hang out in the shallow water. You should see one if you get a chance, while you can, they might not last much longer as a species. Not long ago I saw a bunch of at least fifteen going along. You usually see six or eight. I think they might be banding together to try and survive."

Tab grunted as the bus moved into the left lane to pass a lazy transport truck. The truck driver next to me leaned up and over to see what he could out of the windshield, his road reactions built-in. He soon settled into his seat again, reasonably confident the bus driver knew what he was doing. The back end of the truck we were passing was swaying loosely.

"He's empty, got no load," said Tab.

In a few seconds our seats were adjacent to the driver. Without arm or shoulder movement, his head slowly pivoted to peer over at us, a road-bot inspecting its freeway co-workers. "See how much space is behind the driver? Some of them have a shower and toilet, enough room to make a meal. But basically what you have is a fifty-three-foot box on wheels."

"Must be a strange life," I said.

"I guess so. I s'pose I'd like to have the same route all the time so I could be at home more often. But I don't know about home, anyway."

He scratched his beard and rubbed his face and his cap came up. The bus was dark but I saw his eyes for the first time. They shone like polished gemstones. "I like it well enough. Drive until you're tired, rest, drive until you're tired, rest. When I left yesterday they said that I'd be back, and I will be. It's addictive. You're working but you're moving. And moving kinda puts everything in perspective, the total size, the space between points, the big and small of it all, I guess."

I was curious how the hulking man next to me ever developed a soft spot for manatees, and wondered about the domestic troubles in wait, but soon his head fell to the side and his eyes were closed and I knew that bus sleep was a fragile, precious thing best left alone.

In downtown Tallahassee at 1:00 in the morning the driver made a personal alteration to his arrival announcements. During the five-hour stretch from Mobile, he had built a rapport with some of the passengers. The intercom buzzed to life.

"Okay, folks," he said. "We're just about done. You know, sometimes I wonder, pulling into a city in the middle of the night, what I'll see back there when the lights come on. I've thought about calling *America's Most Wanted* and saying 'I've got all your boys sitting right behind me. Come and get 'em.'"

Muffled comments and laughter filtered along the length of the bus.

"How 'bout sharing some of that catfish now?" said the loudest voice.

The driver snorted. "No chance!" We wheeled into the station. "Here we are, folks. Thanks for a good ride."

I marched away from the foul exhaust of the station and into the livably cool night. The air was moist. The trees were rich. This was not the kind of November I was familiar with.

30

Not knowing what to do on the day Americans were voting for their next president, I loitered in a public space. Specifically, I was at a reading table at Tallahassee's central library. Whether instructing an attitude or merely reflecting one, *The Tallahassee Democrat* front-page headline was big and bold. *Close Race—Anybody Care?*

"I do," said a woman sitting two chairs down from me. There was no one between us. She had looked over and scanned the title as I did. "Sorry, just speaking my mind."

I set the paper down. "Have you chosen your horse in this race?"

"They're both nags if you ask me." She turned back to the coil-bound notebook on the table front of her, scratched out a word or two and added a few new ones. A single edited line for every tangle of thought.

"Do you like to write here?" I asked.

"Sometimes. It's peaceful but populated. I like looking at people."

"Is it working today?"

"I'm not sure," she said. "Feels strange, actually, like I'm describing things I can't see."

"That could be good. Use some different muscles."

"Yeah. I suppose. I wonder if there's a difference, anyway. Sight is subjective—right?—a matter of interpretation, so in a way whatever we're looking at is imagined to begin with. Somehow."

A twitchy old man who excelled at avoiding eye contact was poised over a broadsheet across from us. He cleared his throat with an obvious extra growl. The poet said she still had to vote. After hearing enough of my story to understand why I might like a peek at the inner workings of American democracy, she invited me to come along. We left the old man in peace.

The poet was black and petite and wearing a burnt orange ankle-length dress and two sets of wooden beads. A bright yellow scarf held her wild curly hair away from her face. I decided that she was a sorceress of some kind and, as the tall pack-heavy guy wearing the feathered hat, I was her monstrous medieval sidekick. We were heading for an intersection of four-lane streets.

"Up here you'll be able to witness the madness first-hand," she said. "It's pretty pathetic, actually. Which man to choose doesn't seem to be the most important question. How can we take better control of our own lives? How can we involve ourselves in the lives around us? We need to change the way we treat each other."

Enthusiastic sign-holders were occupying space on all four curbs. Some paced back and forth like they were on strike while others waved madly as though trying to convince people to pull over for a charity car wash. Some of the passing drivers honked. A young guy with a thick beard stood stoically away from the candidate cliques with his handmade placard. *End Sanctions Against Iraq.* As we watched, a blow-dried head popped from the passenger side window of a silver jeep. "Saddam's a fuckin' piece of shit, asshole!" The bearded guy turned and looked at us with a smile and a shrug.

The poet waited patiently as I squeezed a few words from the mob. One sign holder had been on the case since 6:00 a.m., ten hours earlier. I suggested that he was pretty dedicated.

"Oh, I don't know," he said. "Not really. Trillions of our dollars are being spent in certain ways. I'd say there's sufficient self-interest to get involved." He reset his frozen smile and continued to wave robotically at those who barely gave him a glance, an anonymous monarch watching the parade.

"Have there been any problems standing so close to the enemy?"

"It's been a little heated, but fun," he said. "The Democrats surrounded me a couple times, wagging their signs on both sides. I had to call in the cavalry, heh heh."

The Green Party's lone picketer looked weary.

"Some guy threw a can of soda at me," she said. "I guess that was his statement, his contribution to the greater good. I don't understand why we think we have to say, 'They're both bums but they're the best we've got.' Abraham Lincoln was a third-party candidate, you know."

Lincoln's face was engraved above the front doors of the elementary school where the poet was registered to vote. Two paintings adorned opposite walls in the front hallway: one of a space shuttle launching, with flames billowing below and the support structures falling away; the other of men on the moon, with footprints all around them and a flagpole propped nearby in the grey dust. The paintings had obviously been bought as a pair, as images of collective achievement. Behind a long fold-out table a girl of twelve or so earnestly distributed stars-and-stripes stickers that said *I voted!*

"It's kinda funny," said the poet when she returned from the task. "For a few weeks every four years people think they're making a difference."

"Do you feel empowered?"

"Actually, I feel like I got a glimpse of something that's beyond any one of us. The opposite of what they say, every vote counts or whatever. I think the vote is a convincing illusion of individual influence."

As we walked away from the school she decided to roll out the filthy shag carpet. "Do you need a place to crash? I don't have a couch, but I have a floor, and you don't look like someone who would be picky."

"It's all a mattress to me," I said.

The poet lived kitty-corner to the governor of Florida, Jeb Bush, who happened to be the brother of one of the presidential candidates. We walked along the backside of his estate. Near a glass-roofed cabana we could hear the bubbling commotion of a water fountain. Its frothy zenith was visible above the red brick wall perimeter. The only spot that allowed a clear view of the mansion was the point of entry (or point of refusal); a red button intercom was available for those prepared to explain themselves. We stopped to look through the iron gates. Ionic columns fronted the house. In the middle of the curving drive was a recently watered half-moon of greener grass.

The poet put one hand around a vertical bar. "There's this big parade in Tallahassee, and for years the marshal was some guy dressed up like Andrew Jackson. Eventually Native Americans were protesting, spoiling the fun with another view of history."

"Did they delete the Andrew Jackson?"

"I think they moved him to the middle," she said. "Murderous bastard. People don't even know what they're celebrating. Whatever brought us to this point in time is okay by them. 'Hey, a parade! Let's go and cheer!'" She took a deep breath and released it. "Sorry, but the men who started this country wore silk stockings and had slaves. And I'm not sure how much has changed with those the country was handed to. The mirage of America excuses the reality."

She occupied one unit in a subdivided house, an old and worn brownstone set back from the lane in a tangle of overgrown shrubbery. As I trailed her up a dank, dimly lit stairway to the second floor she told me she had been robbed a couple of weeks before.

"I think I know who it was," she said, her keys pointed at the dirty white door. She shrugged. "He was probably desperate for a fix. I'm glad I wasn't here to get in his way."

As far as she knew he had only taken the portable stereo and a stack of CDs; most of what her apartment contained was above the desires of a crook. She had a chair and desk, some throw cushions, and books that were piled by the dozen from the ground up. The floor was almost entirely papered with loose-leaf unfinished poems.

We climbed over a windowsill dripping with candle wax onto a small tarpaper balcony. Although it didn't have a railing of any kind, it did offer a thin, tree-pinched view of the governor's place.

"I can see you but you can't see me," she said, framing the slice of mansion between thumb and index finger.

The poet was about my vintage. "How long have you been writing?" I asked.

"As long as I've been reading. Writing is the only way I'm productive. My sister works for an insurance company in New Hampshire. She's the success. She's my parents' pride; I'm my parents' dilemma. They don't know what happened to me."

Inspired by my show of interest, she grabbed a folder from inside and read me one of her recent poems. "The Sweetest Luxury," it was called. When she was done she lit a clove cigarette and sat back in peace. The poet fed herself by working part-time at an independent bookstore. She had a shift that evening, but she gave me directions to the club where friends were to meet her later.

Having relieved myself of my backpack, I wandered back into Tallahassee, sensing the confused spirit of a national drama. The Democrat-sponsored results watch was held in a lowly community hall with poor ventilation. I made a beeline to the refreshments table, and quickly found myself surrounded by malcontents.

"Is that some kinda dip? What are we supposed to dip with?"

"Is there ice? This pop's a bit warm."

"No beer? I bet the Republicans have beer."

The tiny flag on the end of each toothpick was apparently small consolation for these shortcomings. I filled a paper plate with meatballs, crackers, and cheese and found a seat next to a sweaty obese man wearing a sticker-plastered foam hat. He was leaning forward a little and breathing heavily, his hands stacked on top of a cane.

"It'll be close but I think it'll be ours," he said. "It's up to the west coast."

The county commissioner, an incumbent Democrat who had won again, stood at the end of the room serving quotes to various local journalists. In his left hand was a book called *Imagine What America Could Be In The Twenty-First Century*, and in his right the hands of various people who interrupted the interview to congratulate him. A TV reporter with a surgically altered face waited anxiously for a turn. She kept glancing at her wristwatch, probably wondering why two minutes had to cost her several hours. Using his free hand, her heavy, bearded cameraman was coolly enjoying a complimentary half-sandwich.

A cheer that started in an adjacent room where the latest news was showing on a big screen spread through the crowd like a breaking wave.

"We took Pennsylvania! We took Pennsylvania!"

It was a tight race, as predicted; attention immediately switched to the remaining states.

"Wisconsin is a big one. Important."

"Yeah. So's Utah, and Nevada; Nevada's big."

And then the murmurs carried bad news, which spread quietly but just as quickly as the good.

"Oh. They're not sure about Pennsylvania anymore."

"Man. This could take a while."

After two hours of that nervous back-and-forthing, I headed for the club. It was almost midnight and the place was still easing toward full capacity and full volume. The room was large and faintly lit with purple fluorescent rods, like an unnatural dusk. Televisions loomed over the bar, flashing numbers that kept changing; the overtime anchors were looking more tired than interested. I ordered a beer and continued to eavesdrop.

"They didn't talk about anything that matters to me."

"I hated having to vote against the guy I dislike most."

"Better than voting for the guy you think's gonna win. But yeah, it's bullshit. It's like betting on a football game."

And my favourite, shouted from one friend to another: "If that motherfucker gets in, he better not come shaking hands in my neighbourhood!"

The club was an arena of the active and agile, where energy flowed unimpeded and all accounting of time fell away. I took a place on the outskirts of the dance floor and soon spotted the poet among the vibrating humanity. She had claimed a little space in the approximate centre. Her sandals were off, her bare feet pounding out a rhythm on the dark and sticky hardwood. When she saw me, she waved and smiled and started to dance a little faster. During the very brief calm between songs, she gestured for me to enter the fray. I smiled, saluted her with my bottle of beer, and remained just where I was.

31

Temporarily marooned in Gainesville, I sat on a bench outside the terminal, looking straight ahead through my orange-tinted sunglasses. At frequent intervals, I scratched: I had developed matching rashes around my elbows. Florida was making me sweat.

Along the bench, a girl of perhaps twenty was talking to an old bob-haired woman. "Drug possession," the girl was saying. "They put all three of us away. Bang bang bang. My oldest brother got nine years. Billy, in the middle, he got five. I'm the youngest. Two years. Least we weren't sellin'." She stopped to light a cigarette. "I'm the lucky one," she said, exhaling. "Like, I'm here now."

In a parkette across the street, a cop was standing over a homeless man who appeared to be sleeping. The cop was writing a ticket. He crouched and placed the piece of paper on the man's chest: the cost of loitering.

The bus to Miami via Orlando was announced. I towed my pack to the side of the correct vehicle, and stepped aboard. The journey had taken on a new velocity. What was the rush? I wasn't sure. But I greeted with enthusiasm the notion of winding for hours through Florida's sunburned green, sitting next to a shaded window with a fan's perpetual coolness on my skin.

Great girders of light angled skyward over the circus sprawl known as Orlando. The beams sashayed east and west, north and south, no doubt landing assistance for incoming aliens. As humankind's representative, Mickey Mouse would be sent to make their acquaintance. *Welcome*, he would squeak, extending a furry hand in greeting. *May I escort you to our gift shop?*

I felt becalmed at 4:30 a.m. in Greater Miami. The station was a half-size people depot, far from the city and adjacent to the airport. Buses went no further at this ugly hour. I wouldn't be able to get downtown, or to the beach, until after 6:00. I stood near the wall, deciding if one vacant plastic chair was in any way more enticing than another. A security guard entered the sitting area and scrutinized the room. He immediately spotted a young woman petting her dog, a sad-eyed mongrel, and walked over to her.

"S'cuse me, miss. S'at dog going with you?"

"Yes."

"Don't know if that's allowed."

"I cleared it with them," she said. "I cleared it in Memphis and I cleared it in New Orleans and I cleared it here."

He looked over at the ticket agent, who waved his hand. "Awright then."

I sidled over to the woman and, kneeling next to the dog, started the conversation with the usual mistake. "What's his name?"

"Her name is Ginger."

"Are you tired of getting harassed about her?"

"Yes."

"Have you travelled with her before?"

"Yes."

"What does she think of the bus?"

"She likes it."

Ginger looked as bored and dissatisfied as her owner. The interview was over. The interminable stretch after midnight was the most miserable time to inhabit space with a miserable collection of people. Across from me on the facing row of seats was a young couple with their accidental child, a circumstance, I soon realized, that had also bred self-pity and anger. Whoever wasn't holding the baby at any given time had his or her eyes closed tightly.

"C'mere, brat," said the father, a man in his twenties with bony forearms covered in black and blue tattoos. He grabbed the kid. "Why the hell you cryin' for?"

I left that little tragedy behind, and went to get some air. More youthful parenting was in progress outside. A teenage girl was sitting on a bench beneath the passing furious sound of an occasional jet landing. An infant was in a carrier at her feet. While mixing water and powdered formula she rocked the blanketed baby with one foot. She was also managing to enjoy a cigarette—*look ma, no hands!*—squinting as the smoke curled into her eyes.

Eventually, I returned inside and sat down. In a lucid dream-like state, I followed a trail of minute details. A boy was turning the water fountain on and off, watching intently as the silver-blue arc appeared and disappeared, appeared and disappeared. He tapped the shoulder of the man sitting closest, wanting an audience for his water trick. The man waved him off, said something I couldn't hear. On his other side, a man was finger-drawing the infinity pattern on the bare knee of a woman. The woman's lifeless eyes were turned away, seemingly focused on the heaving belly of the snoring fat man on her other side. Between the feet of the sleeping man, a cockroach was poised at attention, sensing a fallen morsel nearby. With antennae quivering, it moved quickly and directly as only cockroaches can, crashing greedily into the raisin in case hungry competitors had caught the same scent and would be arriving soon. I listened to the man snoring. I chewed raisins, being careful not to drop another.

The schematics of a bus station resemble those of a mind at rest. Engagement with the dizzying universe has been suspended, leaving the precise and nearby points to battle for attention. Lacking diversion, I sought value, I sought allusion. Did the fountain boy signify youthful awe? Were the woman's eyes indicating dead passion? Did the movements of a keen insect suggest that survival involved searching?

Yes, yes, and why the hell not. Even cockroaches were worth more than their weight in meaning.

32

The old man next to me on the boardwalk was pointing up at the blinding-blue sky over Miami Beach.

"See that?" he said. A jumbo jet grumbled west toward the airport. "That's a big one. Just watch. About two of those from that direction every three minutes, lining up to land like they're at the grocery checkout."

The man's name was Winston Crandini. He and I were sitting away from the water on a wooden bench under the limited shade of a palm tree. Crandini was proud of his sedentary lifestyle, content to spend the afternoon confirming that today resembled yesterday. "I drop my ass here at 1:00 and I don't move until 4:00," he said. "But I'm not lazy with my health. I don't drink. I go to bed early. You gotta take care of yourself, like this gal." A thin woman walked by wearing a transparent green scarf wrapped around a string bikini bottom. "Ooh, with the veil over it like that, it's more enticing, you know what I mean?"

The display inspired Crandini to stand and perform a little leg stretching on his end of the bench. He had said he was eighty-three, and gradually I came to believe it. His narrow moustache and what was left of the hair on his head was tinted brown, and he had leathery sagging tits with hard eraser nipples that aimed toward a soft round belly.

Crandini sized me up through his ruby prescription sunglasses. "You don't look like a guy who gets much sun," he said.

"A little is a lot for me."

"Just take it slow," he said. "Let your body adjust. Eventually the darkness will be embedded." Despite his assurances I could feel the afternoon rays bouncing off the white sand and burning my face beneath the rim of my hat. Crandini leaned forward over one stretched leg, not quite touching head to knee. The liver spots on his forehead were like the pattern of rain starting to fall, and in general his skin looked cancerously mottled in uneven shades of brown.

Crandini told me he had spent most of his retired life in the sun. His recent pattern was to split six cheap months between Mexico and Guatemala in order to afford six expensive months in Miami Beach. He said he had a lady in Mexico who did the cooking and cleaning. She was both maid and mistress, I imagined. "She makes these fruit shakes, mango and papaya," he said. "Christ, they're good, one in the morning, maybe one before bed. But, you know, they don't eat unless I'm there. When I'm gone all they have is tortilla chips and hot peppers. When I'm there we get fish or seafood from the market. The arrangement works out pretty well. All I gotta do is pay."

Through his working life Crandini had become an experienced world traveller. He had been an engineer, an international contractor in the steel industry.

"I always wanted to see as much as I could," he said, although his attention was now entirely concentrated on points south of Miami. In my hour with Crandini I learned a little about Jamaica: "Always violent. It comes with the poverty. Christ, they shoot people in the chest, just waste them like rats." And Belize: "You can get all the food they fit on the dish for a dollar. You can buy all the land you can see in any direction for a lousy buck." And Cuba: "Go down there with a bunch of lipstick, some silk stockings, that's all you need. Boys meet you in the streets wanna sell their sisters for a quarter. Can't get any poorer than that. They were starving down there when I was there, selling their bodies for a bar of soap or a potato. A couple of my buddies, Jesus, they were fuckin' 'em like cats. Like *cats.*"

He was getting his shots the following week in preparation for the winter. But he said his blood was strong and he had never fallen prey to disease.

"I gotta slow down, though, you know. The girls were wearing me out." He appraised me again. "Are you looking to meet girls? Women?"

"Not really," I said.

"I just wondered if that's why you came. I'm not a pimp, you know, but I can tell you where to find them. Girls are always hanging around in my lobby looking for a future. From Brazil, Peru, all over, hoping to marry someone so they can stay. They're tired of the life down there, picking beans or pepper or whatever the fuck it is they do for nothing. No hope for them where they are. All these Cubans try to float up here for the same reason. The rules are simple. If they make it onto the soil they can stay; if they're caught on the water they're sent back home."

Those who had come to the promised land flowed before us, a two-way river of pampered flesh: pairs of gay or straight weightlifters (holding hands or not) in snug swim briefs, their bodies chiselled and hairless; their opposites, ex-husbands or escaping husbands with furry shoulders and inner-tubes of waistline fat lapping over extra-large, extra-colourful shorts; women who were perhaps more attractive before they started troubling themselves with the fallacy of flawlessness. A single-engine plane pulled advertising through the sky above the shoreline: GOLD'S GYM—BUY ONE YEAR GET ONE FREE TODAY ONLY.

The sun arrived at a place in its arc where it seemed to be hitting Crandini directly. He leaned back to welcome the heat and light. Two silver chains, one thick and the other thin, were interwoven in his dense grey chest hair.

"My sister says I live like a bum," he said. His eyes were closed. He trusted I was still there, still caring to listen. "She's sitting on a few million bucks, in a rocking chair watching TV. She's gonna have herself a fancy underground condo one of these days, know what I mean? I'm paying six hundred a month here, which isn't living like a bum."

In at least one manner, Crandini was a typical old-timer: when asked, he provided brief and reflexive background. He had gotten married for the first time when he was eighteen ("She was pregnant.") and his second wife had died at childbirth ("The kid lived, she didn't."). Events had become hard little cysts of fact. His son, Winston Crandini II, and his grandson, Winston Crandini III, were both stock-market millionaires. And Winston Crandini IV, his great-grandson, was yet a boy, still easing himself into the legacy.

Crandini opened his eyes to the sight of a middle-aged couple jogging past in choreographed unison. Their sleek, aristocratic Weimaraner ran between them with similar poise.

"Don't these people read the signs?" Crandini barked. "There's one right there. Dogs just running free, shitting all over the place."

A young, single guy slowed toward us on rollerblades, his ankles leaning inward severely. He was singing along nonsensically to the tune playing on his headphones. His cellphone must have vibrated because he fished it out of his deep shorts pocket.

"Yo," he said.

Crandini watched in disdain. "Plus you have to put up with idiots like this. Jesus Christ. Do you believe this guy?"

The rollerblader put his phone away and sat down on a bench perpendicular to ours. "Hey, Crandini, you like this spot or something? You're always here."

"What's the difference? You gotta sit somewhere. The view doesn't change."

The man nodded but looked unconvinced. He spit over his shoulder onto the long grass. Glared down the boardwalk. "I don't know about this strip anymore," he said. "A lot of sick fucks around here, guys having sex, everybody robbing each other. That old man who hangs out by the johns—you know who I'm talking about? The teeth he's still got are yellow and broken and he writes these notes, 'I like big dicks,' or whatever like that. He collects junk, trash, bottles of lotion, whatever he can find."

"You never know what might wash up," said Crandini. But he'd lost the younger man's attention.

"Oh my God. Look...at...those...fucking...tits." He said it with two hands out, fingers facing forward. The woman passed, exposing her backside to us. "C'mon wind, lift that skirt up. Hmm, I think I gotta get some today, get laid, you know, take one of these asses and rip it apart."

Crandini looked at me with a pained smile. *The kid's got it right, I guess, but I wish he didn't have to be so goddamn crude about it.*

The rollerblader stood and began to wobble away. "Awright, Crandini, maybe see you tomorrow."

"His name's Goldman, I think," said Crandini as the man shrank from us. "His father's some kind of merchant in Israel. He gave his kid a hundred grand and he spent it all fast, which isn't hard to do if it's all you're doing. But he's got a mouth on him, you know. Somebody's gonna shut it someday."

The direct sunlight was pulling a strong odour from Crandini's wrinkles and pores. He smelled like bulk cologne. He tapped my right arm with his left hand. A thick gold band centred by a W of tiny diamonds decorated the pinky finger. The ring was sunk in his flesh, never removed. "This as far as you going?"

"I'll probably get to Key West for a few days," I said.

"Not bad," he said. "Still America, though. You have to get into Mexico, Central America. A lot of drifters down there, like you, you know, sleeping on the beach or whatever, you see them with the loaf of bread and tube of salami, living on nothing, but still alive. It's easy to live if that's all you wanna do. You should get down there. Take a bus or whatever. I always tell the young people, 'Get going. Get out of here. It's your world.'"

He said he thought he would be around at least another twenty years, imagined being a crinkled hundred-year-old who watched the planes come in. Toward the end of our conversation Crandini told me his family came from the place where Mussolini was shot. "They strung him up and filled him with bullets," he said. "They have photos of all those guys hanging out, Hitler and Goebbels, the girlfriends, having a picnic by the lake. Christ, they didn't give a shit about the people. Didn't give one shit."

Figuring that I had my fill of his world, I excused myself to take a stroll. Far from the sparkling water a dirt-dark tramp was walking slowly, holding an open Bible below his nose. Next to him an old man in crisp all whites was moving ahead at the same gradual pace, swinging a metal detector over the sand like a pendulum.

33

So these were the Florida Keys, countless islands that divided a gulf and an ocean, globules of earth tied together by turnpike. If Florida was the teat drooping from the underbelly of the union, the Keys were what had dribbled out.

A young couple sprawled across the rear seats of the bus attempted to get a singalong going. I assumed they were hoping to perpetuate the notion of summer, to foster a joint tropical vision: copper stomachs, hammocks built for two, the ice of Cuba Libres melting around a full-moon bonfire. The man was playing an acoustic guitar. The woman crooned. Together they launched into Otis Redding's "(Sittin' on) The Dock of The Bay."

"I left my home in Georgia—"

"Excuse me, folks," said the driver on his tinny p.a. system.

"Headin' for the Frisco Bay—"

"*Folks.*"

The man stopped twanging.

"There are people on board who don't care to hear it."

"Man," said the guitarist. "Killjoy."

The driver buzzed in again. "What was that?"

"Nothing at all," said the young man, calling forward loudly.

"Right, then." *Click.*

Apparently, sunshine was no guarantee of fine moods. Policing was required in paradise. From my usual place in the middle of the bus (where, handily, an ear could face each direction) I watched the silver seas. At the town of Marathon, I began to wonder how much longer it would take. That deadly whimper: *Are we there yet?* Fifty-three miles, according to the road atlas. One more hour. I also wondered at my impatience. Was I simply anxious to lounge again, only in a new location, to arrange my bones on white sand and gauge the lapping of waves? Or did I just want to arrive in order to leave? Did I want this lengthy excursion over with? I didn't think I was eager to return to Canada, where the climate would soon be inhospitable, and where there'd be no hiding from the old question of what to do next. I decided to settle in at Key West as well as possible. Give the end a chance.

At the subsidiary Key West bus depot (again, near the airport), I was startled to meet a Japanese man who said he had begun his own odyssey in Dawson City near the end of the summer. He was sitting on a concrete bench, waiting for the next bus back to Miami. My disbelief of his claim faded as he unfolded a map of North America and laid it across both our laps. We took turns tracing our respective routes. The geography of my recent life was a mess of blue streaks and pink blobs, like the anatomical illustration of some complex creature, a self-contained organism not yet fully understood. I felt removed from the exercise, as though floating above the bench where we sat watching someone's pointed finger slide along various interstates.

My counterpart was about to return to Japan. He had been in the U.S. forty-five days. From the Yukon he went to San Francisco via Vancouver, then across to Chicago, then down through Nashville and Atlanta.

"I do not see United States, I only ride bus," he said. I laughed as a way to agree. He tapped my arm. "At start, no sleep, later, some sleep, now, easy to sleep. But, hmm, still, very tire, very tire. Ready to go Tokyo."

I smiled and nodded. The driver returned from inside the airport terminal with a couple of people who needed passage into downtown Key West. With a shrug I indicated to the Japanese man that I had to board again.

"Yes, yes," he said. "You go."

I waved to him as we pulled away. His trip must also have been a populated chronicle. What notable episodes had unfolded before his eyes? Who were his characters? My appetite for his narrative would, of course, go unfed. Nonetheless, the parallel was a comfort, that I met him at all a remarkable synchronicity. Others had a taste for grand and unpredictable trails. Others had a tendency to move, their motives sometimes puzzling. How many of us were out there?

I am yeti, I thought, yet I am not alone.

34

At any hour of day, the roadways of Key West were clogged with tourist transport. Slight scooters farted beneath the weight of two; droning golf carts easily carried four. Perimeter sounds—a screaming table saw, the rhythmic hammering of nails—were those of growth and renovation. Local industry was trying to keep up with the incoming tide of outside cash.

The town's split personality was most apparent at suppertime. After a long day of sailing, scuba diving, birdwatching, or deep-sea fishing, foot-bound visitors fell gradually from their motel rooms and B & Bs to the sidewalks that led to cloth-napkin dining. Freshened up for a feast, they walked along in pressed slacks and bright cotton blends, shiny and sweet with after-tan lotion.

—I think I got too much sun. I can't believe you let me fall asleep like that. —You looked so peaceful. —Oh well, never mind. Should we try the stone crab tonight?

Local workers, meanwhile, floated in the opposite direction, toward the low-rent district further from the water, their jeans splattered with white paint or black roofing tar, their faces drawn and sweaty, heading for the unlisted open-air bars where drinks were cheap, customers were loyal and wall decor was limited to a few stuffed fish grey with smoke and dust.

As light faded on a Sunday evening, I met a guy who had just spilled from one of those rub-a-dub pubs. I was on the way to a grocery store, my mind running down the usual menu of possible cheap dinners: canned pasta, tuna sandwiches, cold cereal. A man was sitting and leaning against a fence on the other side of a quiet stretch of street away from the downtown area. He was singing some tune until he saw me and focused his attention.

"Hey," he said. "What's happening?"

I waved and kept walking. I was hungry, thinking of the task at hand, in a poor frame of mind for indulging a drunk. Perhaps I already had my fill of despairing booze-fed honesty.

"Where you going in such a rush?" he said.

"To the store," I said, pointing and still walking.

"Hey! C'mon, man." He paused, and his tone changed. "Come over here and *talk* to me," he said.

I stopped. His sadness was too damn authentic. I turned around and crossed the street. His name was Richie. He was in construction. Like most people in town, he wasn't from Key West originally. He was, however, thinking of origins.

"Canada?" he said. "Shit. Guess you didn't see the game then." Richie was drunk-happy that his Eagles had won that afternoon, drunk-sullen that he wasn't in Philadelphia sharing it with someone, anyone. "It woulda bin wild to have bin there." He was slight and seemed shrunken, a middle-aged boy, but also strong as steel. When we shook hands his took to the task like a dependable multi-purpose tool.

"Allow me to be your tour guide," he said, and we started walking along as a pair.

As an older couple was about to pass on our left Richie leaned toward me with an exaggerated whisper. "I'll let ya in on a little secret: you're not supposed to talk to people in this town. Good evening," he said to them. They were short and plump equals. The woman decided against eye contact. "Watch that cholesterol," Richie said over his shoulder.

"It's already too late," said the man, playing along. Richie laughed, buoyed by the audience participation. He crossed to the road side of the walk and waved a hitcher's thumb in front of a passing police cruiser. The cop inside slowed long enough to decide that we weren't worth stopping for. Richie shrugged. "Johnny Lawman is all over this town, keeping things tidy. You get used to it."

His eyes were pinched and bruised with inadequate sleep, but they were trained on the scene's small details. He hadn't been in Key West long, but he wasn't just visiting. "I'm here living the life of probation," he said. "Gotta keep a decent job, find a place to stay, send child support to Philly. Be happy, you know, it's easy. Listen, you got a place to stay? I don't mean anything by it, I'm just opening my door, well it's not really my door cuz I'm staying with this other guy, but he won't think anything of it. He's gay, but, you know, I got no problem, there's a lot of that around here."

As I prepared to gratefully decline the offer (I was ensconced at the international youth hostel), a drag queen sashayed by in a silver wig and red sequin dress. The high-heels were tap-tapping, the cinched butt twisting lightly to the strut.

"Beautiful evening, isn't it?" said Richie.

He'd meant the acknowledgment of the guy as a joke, but the drag queen turned playfully and flashed a great white smile. "Yes, it is. Have a good night, sweetheart."

"Jesus," said Richie. "Did you see that? If you didn't see it too, neither of us would believe it."

A white-haired couple was strolling along across the street, holding hands and smiling at everything at once and nothing in particular.

"Look at that, eh. Bet they've bin together forever and a day. That's the way life should be lived. Filthy rich maybe, but in love."

"A lot of money down here," I said.

"Yeah, there's money here. Shit, this town *is* money. Take a look anywhere. But, you know, a guy can manage for a while at least, no problem making a bit of dough. The elements won't kill you; they'll hurt you now and then, but they won't kill you. And what the fuck, as long as there are hurricanes there will be plenty of work, right?"

"When was the last one?"

"About two years ago. George, I think. We still have work that George gave us, you know, all the flood damage. Something to see, I guess. When it isn't beautiful around here, it's the worst thing you can imagine. I like to believe in the Father, the Son and the Holy Ghost, all right, all the rest just comes, everything else just happens. But you get these storms, they're like reminders, somebody upstairs telling us we don't mean much. I don't know. That was then. This week, next week, next month, sunny and warm, warm and sunny, always the same shit."

"So you miss the snow?"

"Sure, man, why not? Something I know well." The next approaching group of seafood-seekers, two tidy couples, distracted him. He punched my arm: "Let's get some beer—how much do we need, seven, eight bucks?—excuse me, ladies and gentlemen, might we borrow a hundred dollars?" One of the women stopped walking and turned to Richie, who stood with his hands clasped in front and his head cocked to the side. The woman had long bleached blonde hair and breasts like bowling balls in a sack. She laughed loudly and falsely with her mouth wide open and her eyes closed, an obnoxious response to obnoxiousness. A man from the group returned and, without looking at us, ushered away his mate.

Richie swatted at the air behind them. "Ahh, you see, friend, life is shit here. I mean, I put the roofs on all these fucking houses."

Then he was silently standing in place. His nose was pointed at the ground like that of a child expecting to be scolded. I looked at the top of his head, unsure what to do; his longish hair was uncombed and thinning. Eventually Richie looked up again.

"I know I'm drunk. I'm just—listen, my Eagles won 26-23 today in overtime." He stopped, maybe realizing that he had already told me about the football. Maybe he was hard-pressed to celebrate what didn't matter, at the same time as wanting to quietly weep about what did. In a few short minutes I had seen the cycle spin. He was angry because he was frustrated, frustrated because he was sad, sad because something important was missing or long gone or simply never was to begin with. Here to stay, gone to sorrow.

When we started walking again Richie kicked a stone that took flight and rang dully off a parking meter. "I guess, I don't know. I'm lonely. That's all."

I returned to the hostel, thinking I might take notes on the question of solitude. I felt confident that most of my bunkmates would be out somewhere, clanking bottles at one of a hundred Key West tavernas.

When I had arrived in the hostel's courtyard two days earlier I was wearing a T-shirt embroidered with Buddha eyes. One of the employees rushed over.

"Hey, Nepal! I'm from Nepal."

I smiled and put my palms together. *"Namaste,"* I said.

"Namaste." She put a hand on each of my shoulders as though she wanted to hug me but didn't quite have the necessary will. We exchanged generalities about Kathmandu, where she grew up, and the Himalayas. She hadn't been back in three years. I couldn't have been a more slight or indirect tiding from home, but at least I was that.

In my assigned room, assorted half-naked bodies were splayed on the wrinkled grey sheets, young men on holiday or just hiding, each grabbing some rest before or after drinking too much. I stretched out on my bed and entered the fraternity, quickly discovering where the other men hailed from and where they were headed. A guy from Maine was sixty grand in debt and surfing through his vacation on a credit card: "I can pay for it but I can't afford it, know what I mean?" A guy from New Jersey insisted he had no reason to be insecure: "Some guhls have asked to measure the width of my cawk before sex cuz they were worried it would hurt. I'm serious. But seems to me if a baby could come outta there, there's no problem." A Bostonian was suffering from resort-selection malaise: "I don't think there are any good bahs here. I hearda some place called Cocomo, from that song, ya know, I think it's around here. Wherever it is, I'd ratha be there."

Before long I left and went to the communal bathroom. I stood alone in front of the truth-telling joker. *Mirror, mirror, on the wall: Who's the hairiest of them all?* The framework of my chin and cheeks was lost in a thickness of red beard. A blond mane blanketed my ears and shoulders. Not quite Mom's baby anymore. I recalled a brief chat I had with an old woman from New York who sat near me one day on the glassy sands of Miami Beach.

"Why does such a handsome boy like you have a beard like that, and all that hair?" she asked.

I laughed. "How can you be sure that I'm handsome?"

"I can see your eyes, and your smile. You can't hide everything."

My mother would have appreciated the woman's concern. For years, Mom had pleaded with me to look less like a derelict. She yearned for me to be "presentable," I assumed in case I found myself the subject of an impromptu job interview around the next bend in the road. "You don't want to deflect people away from you," she said. I agreed with that. Our exterior determined the guesswork of people we passed on the street. Everyone needed a costume, though, and many were drawn to mine. Drunks, certainly, but in a more general sense, anyone turned out from a life, temporarily or otherwise, anyone desperate to talk.

What was the sum effect of all my listening? Had I grown along with the beard? I could hear the gang behind me, rotating voices, a selection of stunted philosophies concerning sex and finance and politics (a week later and the U.S. election was still a question of angry dispute; no one had yet been declared president).

I returned to the dorm room and reclined on my bunk, content— for a few minutes, anyway—to be an audience for my hostel-mates.

On my third day in town, I went to the beach, intending to take a long walk, perhaps three or four miles. How long was long enough? The same question could be asked of my time in Key West. Should I stay four days? More?

The white sand sloped gently up and away from the shore, and was patterned in long twisted rows. The furthest edge of this damp portion was imprinted with the four-holed paw prints of dogs, and the tiny claw marks of beach birds, designs beyond the reach of waves.

I marched along, adding my own heel gouges to the ornamentation. Before long, I came upon a section of beach busy with patrons spilled from a nearby hotel complex. Suntanners had chosen a side: their eyes were closed looking up, or open looking down reading of romantic adventure. The umbrella-dotted panorama was a vision of respite from life elsewhere, a population relaxed and bare, thinly wrapped in anything other than the usual package of concerns. I passed behind a pair of flabby goddesses. Dark, lined, and sitting cross-legged in loosely strung bikinis, the women resembled chunks of fudge tied with ribbon. One of them raised an arm and pointed over the water. Two fins, one just ahead of the other, had pierced the blue surface about a hundred metres out. In unison the dolphins arced a little and descended, a gradual, graceful curve.

I carried on, alternating between trudging on the hard damp sand and the dry soft, between wearing sandals and not. Despite walking down so many asphalt streets in decent shoes, I felt unprepared, inexperienced. I was slogging along clumsily, the sun a searing weight on my shoulders. Eventually I stopped and sat down on the hot sand.

Staring toward Cuba, I couldn't believe it was over. I had reached the arbitrary finish line. A subsequent race was imminent, of course. If I stayed in Key West a week, another two weeks would remain on my U.S. bus pass; I would use them both to get back to Canada. First I had to find again the sensible pace I had abandoned somewhere on the panhandle. Remind myself why the tortoise beat the hare. I realized that Key West was, in part, a place to try and rest up for the travel that would follow.

I was optimistic about the northward jaunt. On the way, there would be the lost and the losers. There would be kindness and cohesion. I might split an egg sandwich with a beggar in Savannah. I might get my hair trimmed in a D.C. ghetto (to arrive home tidier by inches). I might stay a few nights with friends who lived in Shippensburg, Pennsylvania. A blizzard might trap me for days in upstate New York. On the way, there would be tedium and thirst and overheard affection. There would be encounters I couldn't imagine and wouldn't forget.

In time, I stood again and kept walking. The sun could seem less punishing on a body in motion. As long as your sightline continued to shift, there were things to think about other than the intensity of the heat, or how evenly your limbs were getting roasted.

There was the end of the story to think about, sweeping conclusions to try to avoid. I had ridden humanity's carousel, and now it was time to hop off—the music of people ring-a-linging behind me—and rate the animated whirl. I cared to celebrate. I wanted to announce that anyone who walked the earth had grounds to be astounded. Strolling away from Winston Crandini in Miami Beach, for example, I was downright giddy. I had lucked into someone who loved to talk about himself, who needed to be believed. In the only way I could, I had captured an original creep.

There was the physical act of writing to think about. Soon I would have to sit in a room for hours and days at a stretch, secrete myself in order to get the words right. Be both slave and master. It was time to pass sentences based on sensory perception (acting as judge only in extreme cases), time to grasp at insight. I would have to be entertaining, at least. Be honest.

There was much to recollect, from what felt like ages ago.

How was Red Max coping? He knew better than me how to survive.

Did I still have a great-aunt in Calgary? I hoped so.

Was the crocodile lady a living and breathing creature? She would be happy to prove it.

Oh, yeah—that first man who picked me up while I was hitchhiking in Saskatchewan—was his name actually *Miles*? The truth was sometimes perfect.

There was worry. Should I have been paying closer attention? Even at an extended glance, it didn't seem as though there were many answers out there. I saw landforms, police stations, markets, and bus stops. I saw rivers. I saw people. Many of them told me what they were thinking about.

I left the beach, and began to wind through the streets of Key West. At the hostel, I'd do some laundry, and consider ways to minimize the weight of my pack. The trinkets had accumulated, and as they did I couldn't ignore the eventual need to store it all.

Home, I thought (for the hundredth time). Maybe home is only a feeling, a sensation swirling invisibly at your feet, reminding you that you've got somewhere to return to someday. My own undercurrent was pulling me back to Canada.

I couldn't leave quite yet. One couldn't go to Key West without going to Hemingway's estate (at least not one who aspired to write a novel someday that would rival *The Sun Also Rises*). Here was the king-sized bed, with Spanish headboard, on which Ernest rested with his second wife Pauline. There was the porcelain toilet on which Ernest sometimes sat, cramped and brooding. Everywhere were six- and seven-toed cats, sixty of them lazing about the premises, direct descendants of the mutated ones that nuzzled Ernest.

"We don't fix all the cats," said one of the tour guides. "We need to repopulate, maintain the genes, the tradition."

Hemingway's was a fertile estate: orchids heavy with purple blossoms, wide and thick banana leaves, lush papaya, Christmas palms with dense clusters of red seeds. Most of the acreage was cast in overlapping shadows. A steady, single-file line of the curious climbed a set of metal stairs to peek into the writing studio set back from the house. We were literary voyeurs who had come to lend meaning to the mounted deer's head, peeling and filthy, and to the battered trunk and the shelf of books and, of course, the table and chair. *See the knapsack? See the fishing reel?* Thoughts were whispered so as not to disturb the memory of his efforts in the room. (Leaning forward into a sentence that might advance the story. Leaning back to pull on the beard. The pleasure. The erasure.)

Beneath the studio was a bookstore and souvenir shop where one could purchase shot glasses and cat magnets and *The Hemingway Cookbook* and copies of *The Old Man and the Sea* in German (*Der alte Mann und das Meer*) and French (*Le vieil homme et la mer*). A quote from the man himself was pinned prominently to the wall: "And all the legends that he started in his life live on and prosper, unhampered now by his existence."

Next door to the mansion, Ernest's Café offered the Hammingway sandwich (maple ham and Swiss cheese on a kaiser) for those struck by a novelty hunger. And, on the sidewalk out front, an Austrian painter sold watercolours of the estate. His name was George. The pupils of his ice-blue eyes were like pencil dots. Some of his art was lined up and leaning against the stone wall perimeter.

"Mr. Ernest was famous when he lived here, huh, long time before he died," said George. "People wait for him where we stand already, wait for him to go in, come out."

"How do you think he would feel about the souvenirs?"

"Oh, I sink no problem. I sink he enjoyed money, huh, yes, and people too. He was macho, huh, yes, I sink so." He smiled and pointed a wooden brush at me. "Or maybe the cats have him jealous, huh, you sink?"

Before Key West, George had lived in Switzerland, France, and, for two years, Canada. "Long winters, huh. I had two customers already from Inuvik in north territory. Bought one of my sunsets, like this here, huh, to look at it in dark munts, huh, when no daylight. Wall sunset to help in the dark. I sink a good idea."

"What is your favourite place?" I asked him.

"Oh, maybe I don't know so far. I leave here someday, huh, but I don't sink it matters where to go. I am always still George the painter, yes."

Dave the writer said goodbye to George the painter.

That evening I walked by a restaurant necessarily called Papa's. After passing the patio, I stopped. Took two steps back. The eatery's front was partitioned sliding glass that had been shunted aside. I could see into the middle of the dining room. One of the waitresses looked familiar. Was that what's her name? Her long brown hair was tied up, and she was wearing a uniform, but, yes: the Mexican woman from Longpré Guesthouse in New Orleans. The one who was often reclined in the courtyard, laughing, her limbs glistening with lager. Though we hadn't talked much, I remembered her telling me how she took assorted jobs (house painting, short order cooking) to fund her next move. And she had said that even though her money was running out she had no plans to go home to Monterrey.

I shifted my weight from one foot to the other, watched her remove dirty glasses from a table. So. She would be a waitress in Key West—for now. How strange to see her again.

I was standing at one corner of Papa's patio, my left hand on the wooden enclosure. Mere feet, I realized, from a fifty-something couple. The husband cleared his throat noisily and looked at my chest. I complied with his wish, and left them to break a baguette in peace.

The first performance I saw at The Sunset Celebration was a diminutive black man doing backflips. Dr. Juice was a tight collection of muscle packaged in white undershirt, blue shorts, and worn black running shoes, a schoolyard acrobat. His last feat was an impressive set of handstand push-ups. After the show he walked the perimeter of people holding out a cardboard box, taking a collection.

Dr. Juice had many colleagues: a clown encouraging small dogs to jump through large hoops; an Uncle Sam doing tricks with oversized novelty money; a young red-haired bagpiper in full kilt ensemble, breathing earnestly; a muscular black man with hair like baby snakes playing a steel drum. The talent was spread evenly toward the open water, each entertainer earning what he could from a given space of pink, interlocking paving stones.

I followed Dr. Juice to the edge of the parking lot at the land end of the pier. He sat cross-legged on a patch of grass and began to straighten dollar bills. He realized he was being watched. "Not as much paper as yesterday," he said.

"How did you end up in Key West?" I asked.

"I'm a tumbler, man," he said with a gold-toothed smile. He secured the tidy stack of cash with two elastic bands. "I bin tumblin' all over. New York, Texas, California. Bin in the States twenty years now, my home away from home."

He was from Guyana. Neatly enough, I had just read on a seaside information board that pelicans migrated as far south as Guyana to fish in other waters for a few months, returning to Florida in the fall to mate and raise chicks. Neatly enough, a pelican was perched at that moment on a nearby metal railing, cleaning itself.

"One of these days I'll have to stop," said Dr. Juice. "You can't live forever with a suitcase in your hand." He stood and pulled a pair of athletic pants over his shorts. "When you move like me you get tired."

I walked along the pier again. Although a raft of dark cloud had drifted over the falling sun, a thin bar of open space remained between the blob and the horizon. As the ball started to appear below the cloud line, the crowd's attention moved to the water.

Seizing the opportunity for dramatics, the bagpiper started in with "Auld Lang Syne." I stopped near a small family unit. "Honey, look at the sky," said the wife. Her husband was non-responsive, distracted by the nearest performer, a juggler balanced on an eight-foot highwire. Then their young daughter tugged at his pants pocket. "Daddy!" she said. "Look at the sky!" So he did.

The juggler realized he was losing his audience, his wages. One at a time he caught and held his three silver pins. "We're almost done here, folks," he said. He didn't have their ears either. Seeming to give up, he stepped back to the small platform at the end of the wire and looked with the rest of us toward the sea. A couple of sailboats had drifted into view in the near distance. The sun was a ruby disk, muted but still vibrant, easy to admire dead-on and easy to discern when it was entirely gone, and it was gone quickly, a coin dropped into a jukebox.

The crowd disbanded slowly, each tiny fragment deciding in the dusk what to do with itself next. I started to walk away, returning to a stretch of beach I had found that would be mostly vacant at this hour, removing myself briefly from the ongoing carnival of humanity.

When the action was sufficiently behind me, I stopped and found a place to sit. The bank of sand beneath me was still cooling from the day. As I watched colours drain from the sky, I was reminded of a celestial display I had seen back in Dawson City. When we were chatting next to the Yukon River, I had asked Red Max about the northern lights. How common were they? Could their appearance be predicted ahead of time? He shrugged: "Sometimes you just look up, and there they are."

Perhaps that very night, maybe the one after, I had returned to the riverside, walking a short distance away from town. After I got somewhat beyond the glow of Dawson, I had looked up, and there they were, appearing out of the cold, thin air. At first, and suddenly, the sky was a patchwork of vibrating green ribbons that morphed after a minute or two into a single fluid sheet moving like a beach towel being waved, faint stars dotting the fringes like thrown sand; then the full sheet sliced itself into pieces, swaths of painted light that in turn became a giant phosphorescent fan, opening and closing slowly, and around the edges of the fan shot billows of shocking pink as if the sky had embarrassed itself; the final act involved a solid cover of electric lemon-lime that stretched from one horizon to the other. I gazed up like a fish stunned by something shiny on the surface of a tropical lagoon.

Too many details changing too quickly, I had thought then. And I thought it again now, on a curve of beach in Florida, as I watched the most recent of a thousand scenes witnessed since August that I hoped to portray. Not that the sunset before me had many more hues worth describing: a curtain of darkness was closing in fast from the east.

I stood up. It was time to return to the hostel and pack my bag. While brushing sand off my shorts, I felt a weight at my thigh: the compass. Since the most recent reorganization of my backpack, I had been carrying my father's hand-me-down gift in a front pocket. I popped open the slightly tarnished lid. The needle shivered. Perhaps, like the compass, by my very nature I pointed in a particular direction.

Due north, of course: I was due north.

N

About the Author

Dave Cameron grew up in Maple, Ontario, and studied magazine journalism at Ryerson University. A freelance writer, his work has appeared in *The Globe and Mail*, *The Toronto Star*, *The Ottawa Citizen*, and *Cottage Life* magazine, among other publications. He has lived in Vancouver, Toronto, and Halifax, and has travelled in Europe, Asia, and Australia.